God Cares for You

God Cares for You

Richard Dayringer

BROADMAN PRESS
Nashville, Tennessee

DEDICATED
to
Janet
Steve, Dave, Deby, Dan, and James
and the
Patients
Family Members
and
Staff
Baptist Medical Center
Kansas City, Missouri

4252-32
ISBN: 0-8054-5232-X

Dewey Decimal Classificaticn: 242.4
Subject heading: CONSOLATION

Library of Congress Catalog Card Number: 83-70210
Printed in the United States of America

Introduction

Most of the material contained in this book was prepared and used in one way or another with the patients, their families, and the staff at the Baptist Medical Center in Kansas City, Missouri, while I served there as the Director of the Department of Pastoral Care and Counseling from 1965 to 1974. Many of these items were shared at the bedside or in waiting rooms. The meditations and some of the poetry were read as devotional meditations over the hospital paging system. The sermons were given in the hospital chapel services which were also televised on closed-circuit into the patients' rooms.

All of the meditations were printed in the hospital newspaper, *Heartbeat.* Many of the meditations were published in the *Word and Way,* the *Baptist Digest,* and the Missouri and Kansas state Baptist newspapers respectively, under a column headed "Spiritual Rx." A dozen of them were published in the *Illinois Baptist* in an opinion column. Some of the sermons have been delivered in various churches in Missouri, Kansas, and Illinois.

The other group with whom this material has been shared is my wife and our five children.

ACKNOWLEDGMENTS

Grateful acknowledgment for using material from other sources is extended to the following: For "Isolation" by Richard Dayringer to the *Kansas City Star*, September 17, 1967, p. 6D. The poem won first place in the Kansas City Pop Poem Contest sponsored by Simon & Schuster Publishers. For "Gifts" composed or quoted by a hospital "Candy Striper" in a letter to the hospital administration after reaching her eighteenth birthday. For "The Ageless Quest" to Robert Major Mathews, M.D. Used by permission. For "physician," "infection," "a season of darkness," "time, the invisible mender," and "for william edward" to Nancy Sue Pistorius. Used by permission. For "A Prayer for Understanding," "A Prayer During Pain," and "A Prayer for Rest" by Russell L. Dicks to Macmillan Publishing, Co., Inc. from *The Art of Ministering to the Sick* by Russell L. Dicks and Richard C. Cabot, pp. 222-225, 227. Copyright 1936 by Macmillan Publishing Co., Inc., renewed 1964 by Russell L. Dicks. Used by permission. For the ideas in "Wrestling with Illness" to John Patton, "Ministry in Extended Care Facilities," from *Pastor and Patient*, ed. Richard Dayringer, published by Jason Aronson, 1982, pp. 253-261. For the ideas in "Time and the Father" and "Food and Love" to Myron Madden who was my professor in clinical pastoral education at the Southern Baptist Hospital in New Orleans, 1961-1963. For the ideas in "Life's Punctuation Marks" and "The Case of the Cross Collector" to William Jones, a Canadian friend from days at New Orleans Baptist Theological Seminary. Unless otherwise indicated all Scripture references are from the Revised Version of the Bible, copyrighted 1946, 1952, ©1971, 1973. All Scripture references marked KJV are from the King James Version of the Bible. Quotations from *The Living Bible* are used by permission of Tyndale House Publishers, Wheaton, Illinois. ©Tyndale House Publishers, 1971.

Contents

Part I

Comfort
from the Word of God

Afraid

Be strong and of a good courage; be not afraid, neither be thou dismayed: for the Lord thy God is with thee wherever thou goest" (Josh. 1:9, KJV).

In peace I will both lie down and sleep;
    for thou alone, O Lord, makest me dwell in safety
    (Ps. 4:8).

The Lord is my light and my salvation; whom shall I fear? The Lord is the strength of my life; of whom shall I be afraid? . . .
    One thing have I desired of the Lord, that will I seek after; that I may dwell in the house of the Lord all the days of my life, to behold the beauty of the Lord, and to inquire in his temple.
    For in the time of trouble he shall hide me in his pavilion: in the secret of his tabernacle shall he hide me, he shall set me up upon a rock. And now shall mine head be lifted up above mine enemies round about me: therefore will I offer in his tabernacle sacrifices of joy; I will sing, yea, I will sing praises unto the Lord.
    Hear, O Lord, when I cry with my voice: have mercy also upon me, and answer me. When thou saidst, Seek ye my face; my heart said unto thee, thy face, Lord, will I seek. Hide not thy face far from me; put not thy servant away in anger: thou hast been my help; leave me not, neither forsake me, O God of my salvation. When my father and my mother forsake me, then the Lord will take me up (Ps. 27:1,4-10, KJV).

When I am afraid,
    I put my trust in thee.
In God, whose word I praise,
    in God I trust without a fear.
    What can flesh do to me? (Ps. 56:3-4).

We are afflicted in every way, but not crushed; perplexed, but not driven to despair; persecuted, but not forsaken; struck down, but not destroyed; always carrying in the body the death of Jesus, so that the life of Jesus may also be manifested in our bodies. For while we live we are always being given up to death for Jesus' sake, so that the life of Jesus may be manifested in our mortal flesh. So death is at work in us, but life in you.

Since we have the same spirit of faith as he had who wrote, "I believed, and so I spoke," we too believe, and so we speak, knowing that he who raised the Lord Jesus will raise us also with Jesus and bring us with you into his presence. For it is all for your sake, so that as grace extends to more and more people it may increase thanksgiving, to the glory of God.

So we do not lose heart. Though our outer nature is wasting away, our inner nature is being renewed every day. For this slight momentary affliction is preparing for us an eternal weight of glory beyond all comparison, because we look not to the things that are seen but to the things that are unseen; for the things that are seen are transient, but the things that are unseen are eternal (2 Cor. 4:8-18).

He said to me, "My grace is sufficient for you, for my power is made perfect in weakness." I will all the more gladly boast of my weaknesses, that the power of Christ may rest upon me (v. 9).

Hence we can confidently say,
    "The Lord is my helper,
    I will not be afraid;
    what can man do to me?" (Heb. 13:6).

Anxious

God is our refuge and strength, a very present help in trouble. Therefore will not we fear, though the earth should be removed, and though the mountains be carried into the midst of the sea; though the waters thereof roar and be troubled, though the mountains shake with the swelling thereof (Ps. 46:1-3, KJV).

Be still, and know that I am God: I will be exalted among the heathen, I will be exalted in the earth. The Lord of hosts is with us; the God of Jacob is our refuge (vv. 10-11, KJV).

Therefore I tell you, do not be anxious about your life, what you shall eat or what you shall drink, nor about your body, what you shall put on. Is not life more than food, and the body more than clothing? Look at the birds of the air: they neither sow nor reap nor gather into barns, and yet your heavenly Father feeds them. Are you not of more value than they? And which of you by being anxious can add one cubit to his span of life? And why are you anxious about clothing? Consider the lilies of the field, how they grow; they neither toil nor spin; yet I tell you, even Solomon in all his glory was not arrayed like one of these. But if God so clothes the grass of the field, which today is alive and tomorrow is thrown into the oven, will he not much more clothe you, O men of little faith? Therefore do not be anxious, saying, "What shall we eat?" or "What shall we drink?" or "What shall we wear?" For the Gentiles seek all these things; and your heavenly Father knows that you need them all. But seek first his kingdom and his righteousness, and all these things shall be yours as well.

Therefore do not be anxious about tomorrow, for tomorrow will be anxious for itself. Let the day's own trouble be sufficient for the day (Matt. 6:25-34).

Cast all your anxieties on him, for he cares about you (1 Pet. 5:7).

At my first defense no one took my part; all deserted me. May it not be charged against them! But the Lord stood by me and gave me strength to proclaim the message fully, that all the Gentiles might hear it. So I was rescued from the lion's mouth. The Lord will rescue me from every evil and save me for his heavenly kingdom. To him be the glory for ever and ever. Amen (2 Tim. 4:16-18).

Comfort

The eternal God is your dwelling place,
      and underneath are the everlasting arms.
And he thrust out the enemy before you,
      and said, Destroy (Deut. 33:27).

I keep the Lord always before me;
      because he is at my right hand, I shall not be moved
      (Ps. 16:8).

Lord, thou hast been our dwelling place
      in all generations.
Before the mountains were brought forth,
      or ever thou hadst formed the earth and the world,
      from everlasting to everlasting thou art God (Ps. 90:1-2).

I lift up my eyes to the hills.
      From whence does my help come?
My help comes from the Lord,
      who made heaven and earth.

He will not let your foot be moved,
      he who keeps you will not slumber.

Behold, he who keeps Israel
    will neither slumber nor sleep.

The Lord is your keeper;
    the Lord is your shade
    on your right hand.
The sun shall not smite you by day,
    nor the moon by night.

The Lord will keep you from all evil;
    he will keep your life.
The Lord will keep
    your going out and your coming in
    from this time forth and for evermore (Ps. 121:1-8).

He will swallow up death for ever, and the Lord God will wipe away tears from all faces, and the reproach of his people he will take away from all the earth, for the Lord has spoken (Isa. 25:8).

Have you not known? Have you not heard?
The Lord is the everlasting God,
    the Creator of the ends of the earth.
He does not faint or grow weary,
    his understanding is unsearchable.
He gives power to the faint,
    and to him who has no might he increases strength.
Even youths shall faint and be weary,
    and young men shall fall exhausted;
    but they who wait for the Lord shall renew their strength,
    they shall mount up with wings like eagles,
    they shall run and not be weary,
    they shall walk and not faint (Isa. 40:28-31).

As one whom his mother comforts,
    so I will comfort you;
    you shall be comforted in Jerusalem (Isa. 66:13).

Blessed are they that mourn: for they shall be comforted (Matt. 5:4, KJV).

I will not leave you comfortless: I will come to you. Yet a little while, and the world seeth me no more; but ye see me: because I live, ye shall live also. At that day ye shall know that I am in my Father, and ye in me, and I in you. He that hath my commandments, and keepeth them, he it is that loveth me: and he that loveth me shall be loved of my Father, and I will love him, and will manifest myself to him (John 14:18-21, KJV).

None of us lives to himself, and none of us dies to himself. If we live, we live to the Lord, and if we die, we die to the Lord; so then, whether we live or whether we die, we are the Lord's (Rom. 14:7-8).

Blessed be the God and Father of our Lord Jesus Christ, the Father of mercies and God of all comfort, who comforts us in all our affliction, so that we may be able to comfort those who are in any affliction, with the comfort with which we ourselves are comforted by God (2 Cor. 1:3-4).

For as we share abundantly in Christ's sufferings, so through Christ we share abundantly in comfort too. If we are afflicted, it is for your comfort and salvation; and if we are comforted, it is for your comfort, which you experience when you patiently endure the same sufferings that we suffer. Our hope for you is unshaken; for we know that as you share in our sufferings, you will also share in our comfort.
      For we do not want you to be ignorant, brethren, of the affliction we experienced in Asia; for we were so utterly, unbearably crushed that we despaired of life itself (2 Cor. 1:5-8).

I can do all things in him who strengthens me (Phil. 4:13).

We would not have you ignorant, brethren, concerning those who are asleep, that you may not grieve as others do who have no hope. For since we believe that Jesus died and rose again, even so, through Jesus, God will bring with him those who have fallen asleep (1 Thess. 4:13-14).

Then I saw a new heaven and a new earth; for the first heaven and the first earth had passed away, and the sea was no more. And I saw the holy city, new Jerusalem, coming down out of heaven from God, prepared as a bride adorned for her husband; and I heard a loud voice from the throne saying, "Behold, the dwelling of God is with men. He will dwell with them, and they shall be his people, and God himself will be with them; he will wipe away every tear from their eyes, and death shall be no more, neither shall there be mourning nor crying nor pain any more, for the former things have passed away."

And he who sat upon the throne said, "Behold, I make all things new." Also he said, "Write this, for these words are trustworthy and true." And he said to me, "It is done! I am the Alpha and the Omega, the beginning and the end. To the thirsty I will give from the fountain of the water of life without payment. He who conquers shall have this heritage, and I will be his God and he shall be my son (Rev. 21:1-7).

Conscience Stricken

Come now, let us reason together,
    says the Lord:
though your sins are like scarlet,
    they shall be as white as snow;
though they are red like crimson,
    they shall become like wool (Isa. 1:18).

The true light that enlightens every man was coming into the world (John 1:9).

There was a man of the Pharisees, named Nicodemus, a ruler of the Jews: The same came to Jesus by night, and said unto him, Rabbi, we know that thou art a teacher come from God: for no man can do these miracles that thou doest, except God be with him. Jesus answered and said unto him, Verily, verily, I say unto thee, Except a man be born again, he cannot see the kingdom of God (John 3:1-3, KJV).

He who believes in him is not condemned; he who does not believe is condemned already, because he has not believed in the name of the only Son of God (John 3:18).

For every one who does evil hates the light, and does not come to the light, lest his deeds should be exposed (v. 20).

Crisis

Trust in the Lord with all thine heart; and lean not unto thine own understanding. In all thy ways acknowledge him, and he shall direct thy paths (Prov. 3:5-6, KJV).

For God hath not given us the spirit of fear; but of power, and of love, and of a sound mind (2 Tim. 1:7, KJV).

For we have not a high priest who is unable to sympathize with our weaknesses, but one who in every respect has been tempted as we are, yet without sin. Let us then with confidence draw near to the throne of grace, that we may receive mercy and find grace to help in time of need (Heb. 4:15-16).

Discouraged

Fret not yourself because of the wicked,
　　be not envious of wrongdoers!
For they will soon fade like the grass,
　　and wither like the green herb.

Trust in the Lord, and do good;
　　so you will dwell in the land, and enjoy security.
Take delight in the Lord,
　　and he will give you the desires of your heart.

Commit your way to the Lord;
　　trust in him, and he will act.
He will bring forth your vindication as the light,
　　and your right as the noonday.

Be still before the Lord, and wait patiently for him;
　　fret not yourself over him who prospers in his way,
　　over the man who carries out evil devices!

Refrain from anger, and forsake wrath!
　　Fret not yourself; it tends only to evil (Ps. 37:1-8).

Why are you cast down, O my soul,
　　and why are you disquieted within me?
Hope in God; for I shall again praise him,
　　my help and my God (Ps. 42:11).

Blessed are you when men revile you and persecute you and utter all kinds of evil against you falsely on my account. Rejoice and be glad, for your reward is great in heaven, for so men persecuted the prophets who were before you (Matt. 5:11-12).

"Let not your hearts be troubled; believe in God, believe also in me. In my Father's house are many rooms; if it were not so, would I have told you that I go to prepare a place for you? And when I go and prepare a place for you, I will come again and will take you to myself, that where I am you may be also. And you know the way where I am going." Thomas said to him, "Lord, we do not know where you are going; how can we know the way?" Jesus said to him, "I am the way, and the truth, and the life; no one comes to the Father, but by me. If you had known me, you would have known my Father also; henceforth you know him and have seen him."

Philip said to him, "Lord, show us the Father, and we shall be satisfied." Jesus said to him, "Have I been with you so long, and yet you do not know me, Philip? He who has seen me has seen the Father; how can you say, 'Show us the Father'? Do you not believe that I am in the Father and the Father in me? The words that I say to you I do not speak on my own authority; but the Father who dwells in me does his works. Believe me that I am in the Father and the Father in me; or else believe me for the sake of the works themselves" (John 14:1-11).

Disillusioned

I believe that I shall see the goodness of the Lord
    in the land of the living!
Wait for the Lord;
    be strong, and let your heart take courage;
    yea, wait for the Lord! (Ps. 27:13-14).

Commit your way to the Lord;
    trust in him, and he will act.
He will bring forth your vindication as the light,
    and your right as the noonday.

Be still before the Lord, and wait patiently for him;
    fret not yourself over him who prospers in his way,
    over the man who carries out evil devices! (Ps. 37:5-7).

And whenever you stand praying, forgive, if you have anything against any one; so that your Father also who is in heaven may forgive you your trespasses (Mark 11:25).

Therefore lift your drooping hands and strengthen your weak knees, and make straight paths for your feet, so that what is lame may not be put out of joint but rather be healed. Strive for peace with all men, and for the holiness without which no one will see the Lord. See to it that no one fail to obtain the grace of God; that no "root of bitterness" spring up and cause trouble, and by it the many become defiled (Heb. 12:12-15).

Facing a Crisis

I called upon the Lord in distress: the Lord answered me, and set me in a large place. The Lord is on my side; I will not fear: what can man do unto me? The Lord taketh my part with them that help me: therefore shall I see my desire upon them that hate me. It is better to trust in the Lord than to put confidence in man (Ps. 118:5-8, KJV).

I will bless the Lord at all times;
    his praise shall continually be in my mouth.
My soul makes its boast in the Lord;
    let the afflicted hear and be glad.
O magnify the Lord with me,
    and let us exalt his name together! (Ps. 34:1-3).

This poor man cried, and the Lord heard him,
    and saved him out of all his troubles (v. 6).

The salvation of the righteous is from the Lord;
    he is their refuge in the time of trouble.

The Lord helps them and delivers them;
    he delivers them from the wicked, and saves them,
    because they take refuge in him (Ps. 37:39-40).

Now I know that the Lord will help his anointed;
    he will answer him from his holy heaven
    with mighty victories by his right hand.
Some boast of chariots, and some of horses;
    but we boast of the name of the Lord our God.
They will collapse and fall;
    but we shall rise and stand upright.

Give victory to the king, O Lord;
    answer us when we call (Ps. 20:6-9).

Fearful

For I, the Lord your God,
    hold your right hand;
    it is I who say to you, "Fear not,
    I will help you" (Isa. 41:13).

But the Comforter, which is the Holy Ghost, whom the Father
will send in my name, he shall teach you all things, and bring all
things to your remembrance, whatsoever I have said unto you.
Peace I leave with you, my peace I give unto you: not as the
world giveth, give I unto you. Let not your heart be troubled,
neither let it be afraid (John 14:26-27, KJV).

I am sure that neither death, nor life, nor angels, nor prin-
cipalities, nor things present, nor things to come, nor powers,
nor height, nor depth, nor anything else in all creation, will be
able to separate us from the love of God in Christ Jesus our Lord
(Rom. 8:38-39).

So we do not lose heart. Though our outer nature is wasting away, our inner nature is being renewed every day. For this slight momentary affliction is preparing for us an eternal weight of glory beyond all comparison, because we look not to the things that are seen but to the things that are unseen; for the things that are seen are transient, but the things that are unseen are eternal (2 Cor. 4:16-18).

Let all men know your forbearance. The Lord is at hand. Have no anxiety about anything, but in everything by prayer and supplication with thanksgiving let your requests be made known to God. And the peace of God, which passes all understanding, will keep your hearts and your minds in Christ Jesus (Phil. 4:6-7).

Guidance in Time of Decision

If any of you lacks wisdom, let him ask God, who gives to all men generously and without reproaching, and it will be given him. But let him ask in faith, with no doubting, for he who doubts is like a wave of the sea that is driven and tossed by the wind (Jas. 1:5-6).

In Temptation

Now to him who is able to keep you from falling and to present you without blemish before the presence of his glory with rejoicing, to the only God, our Savior through Jesus Christ our Lord, be glory, majesty, dominion, and authority, before all time and now and for ever. Amen (Jude 24-25).

Blessed is the man who endures trial, for when he has stood the test he will receive the crown of life which God has promised to those who love him (Jas. 1:12).

Finally, brethren, whatever is true, whatever is honorable, whatever is just, whatever is pure, whatever is lovely, whatever is gracious, if there is any excellence, if there is anything worthy of praise, think about these things (Phil. 4:8).

There hath no temptation taken you but such as is common to man: but God is faithful, who will not suffer you to be tempted above that ye are able; but will with the temptation also make a way to escape, that ye may be able to bear it (1 Cor. 10:13, KJV).

Joy

Truly, truly, I say to you, you will weep and lament, but the world will rejoice; you will be sorrowful, but your sorrow will turn into joy (John 16:20).

So you have sorrow now, but I will see you again and your hearts will rejoice, and no one will take your joy from you. In that day you will ask nothing of me. Truly, truly, I say to you, if you ask anything of the Father, he will give it to you in my name. Hitherto you have asked nothing in my name; ask, and you will receive, that your joy may be full (vv. 22-24).

The joy of the Lord is your strength (Neh. 8:10, KJV).

Rejoice with joy unspeakable and full of glory (1 Pet. 1:8, KJV).

Needing Inward Peace

The meek shall possess the land,
    and delight themselves in abundant prosperity.

Mark the blameless man, and behold the upright,
    for there is posterity for the man of peace (Ps. 37:11,37).

Let me hear what God the Lord will speak,
    for he will speak peace to his people,
    to his saints, to those who turn to him in their hearts
    (Ps. 85:8).

Thou wilt keep him in perfect peace,
    whose mind is stayed on thee: because he trusteth in thee
    (Isa. 26:3, KJV).

Therefore, since we are justified by faith, we have peace with God through our Lord Jesus Christ. Through him we have obtained access to this grace in which we stand, and we rejoice in our hope of sharing the glory of God. More than that, we rejoice in our sufferings, knowing that suffering produces endurance, and endurance produces character, and character produces hope, and hope does not disappoint us, because God's love has been poured into our hearts through the Holy Spirit which has been given to us (Rom. 5:1-5).

Let the peace of Christ rule in your hearts, to which indeed you were called in the one body. And be thankful (Col. 3:15).

Needing Prayer

This is the confidence which we have in him, that if we ask
anything according to his will he hears us. And if we know that
he hears us in whatever we ask, we know that we have obtained
the requests made of him (1 John 5:14-15).

The Lord answer you in the day of trouble!
The name of the God of Jacob protect you!
May he send you help from the sanctuary,
     and give you support from Zion!
May he remember all your offerings,
     and regard with favor your burnt sacrifices!
May he grant you your heart's desire,
     and fulfil all your plans!
May we shout for joy over your victory,
     and in the name of our God set up our banners!
May the Lord fulfil all your petitions! (Ps. 20:1-5).

Make me to know thy ways, O Lord;
     teach me thy paths.
Lead me in thy truth, and teach me,
     for thou art the God of my salvation;
     for thee I wait all the day long.

Be mindful of thy mercy, O Lord,
     and of thy steadfast love,
     for they have been from of old.
Remember not the sins of my youth,
     or my transgressions;
     according to thy steadfast love, remember me,
     for thy goodness' sake, O Lord! (Ps. 25:4-7).

Again I say to you, if two of you agree on earth about anything they ask, it will be done for them by my Father in heaven (Matt. 18:19).

Why are you cast down, O My soul,
    and why are you disquieted within me?
Hope in God; for I shall again praise him,
    my help and my God (Ps. 42:5).

Likewise the Spirit helps us in our weakness; for we do not know how to pray as we ought, but the Spirit himself intercedes for us with sighs too deep for words. And he who searches the hearts of men knows what is the mind of the Spirit, because the Spirit intercedes for the saints according to the will of God.
For we know that in everything God works for good with those who love him, who are called according to his purpose (Rom. 8:26-28).

Pain

Blessed is he who considers the poor!
The Lord delivers him in the day of trouble;
    the Lord protects him and keeps him alive;
    he is called blessed in the land;
    thou dost not give him up to the will of his enemies.
The Lord sustains him on his sickbed;
    in his illness thou healest all his infirmities.

As for me, I said, "O Lord, be gracious to me;
    heal me, for I have sinned against thee!" (Ps. 41:1-4).

For we have not an high priest which cannot be touched with the feeling of our infirmities; but was in all points tempted like as we are, yet without sin (Heb. 4:15, KJV).

And God shall wipe away all tears from their eyes; and there shall be no more death, neither sorrow, nor crying, neither shall there be any more pain: for the former things are passed away (Rev. 21:4, KJV).

Rest in Time of Weariness

"Come to me, all who labor and are heavy laden, and I will give you rest. Take my yoke upon you, and learn from me; for I am gentle and lowly in heart, and you will find rest for your souls. For my yoke is easy, and my burden is light" (Matt. 11:28-30).

The Lord is my shepherd; I shall not want. He maketh me to lie down in green pastures: he leadeth me beside the still waters. He restoreth my soul: he leadeth me in the paths of righteousness for his name's sake.

Yea, though I walk through the valley of the shadow of death, I fear no evil: for thou art with me; thy rod and thy staff, they comfort me.

Thou preparest a table before me in the presence of mine enemies: thou anointest my head with oil; my cup runneth over.

Surely goodness and mercy shall follow me all the days of my life: and I will dwell in the house of the Lord for ever (Ps. 23, KJV).

Sleep

In peace I will both lie down and sleep;
  for thou alone, O Lord, makest me dwell in safety
  (Ps. 4:8).

By day the Lord commands his steadfast love;
  and at night his song is with me,
  a prayer to the God of my life (Ps. 42:8).

Thankful

Praise the Lord, all nations!
  Extol him, all peoples!
For great is his steadfast love toward us;
  and the faithfulness of the Lord endures for ever.
Praise the Lord! (Ps. 117).

This is the Lord's doing;
  it is marvelous in our eyes.
This is the day which the Lord has made;
  let us rejoice and be glad in it.
Save us, we beseech thee O Lord!
  O Lord, we beseech thee give us success! (Ps. 118:23-25).

Make a joyful noise to the Lord, all ye lands!
Serve the Lord with gladness!
Come before his presence with singing!

Know that the Lord he is God: it is he that hath made us, and not
we ourselves; we are his people, and the sheep of his pasture.

Enter into his gates with thanksgiving, and his courts with praise: Be thankful unto him, and bless his name.

For the Lord is good; his mercy is everlasting; and his truth endureth to all generations (Ps. 100, KJV).

Give thanks in all circumstances; for this is the will of God in Christ Jesus for you (1 Thess. 5:18).

Through him then let us continually offer up a sacrifice of praise to God, that is, the fruit of lips that acknowledge his name (Heb. 13:15).

R.R. Hester

Part II

Thoughts to Strengthen

Sing in a Strange Land?

A farm family decided to move to the city. On their last day on the farm, their preschool boy spent the day telling the various animals and buildings good-bye. He told the horse, "Good-bye, I'm moving to the city." He made the rounds, telling the cows, the chickens, the sheep, and the pigs good-bye. That night, he knelt beside his bed and prayed, "Good-bye, God, I'm moving to the city."

When the Israelites were taken away captives from their Promised Land of Palestine, they felt they were being removed from the care and presence of God. They were dispersed over many parts of the earth and, of course, they were grief stricken and depressed about it. The psalmist raised this issue for us when he asked how he could possibly sing the Lord's song in a strange land: "How shall we sing the Lord's song in a foreign land?" (Ps. 137:4).

Yet the Hebrew children discovered a new truth about God as a result of their often being forcibly abducted from their homes. They learned that God was still with them wherever they went, even in a strange land. It was an important lesson for them to learn, and they have passed it on to us.

There are some parallels between what happened to the Israelites and what happens to a patient today who goes to the hospital. Like the Israelites, he is forced to go to a strange place for a while. It looks, sounds, and smells differently from anything he has ever known. The natives of that strange land

30

called the hospital seem almost to speak a foreign language as they talk in complicated medical terminology. The patient feels a sense of separation and loneliness from his own people whom he loves most and is surrounded by strangers in color-coded uniforms. The patient, too, may feel isolated and abandoned. He may ask with the psalmist, "How could I sing and be happy in this weird place?"

But patients can discover for themselves what the Israelites discovered for themselves—that God still cares for us and is present with us wherever we are. And through God's comfort and love the patient can find happiness and sing the hymns of God in Christ. These may well help him to endure his illness, to cooperate with the ministry of the healing team and to emerge healthy enough once again to return to his own land.

> All people that on earth do dwell,
> Sing to the Lord with cheerful voice;
> Him serve with fear, his praise forthtell;
> Come ye before him and rejoice.

> —WILLIAM KETHE

The Eternal Friend

If ever there is a time in life when we need the support of friends, it is during illness. Illness has a way of isolating its victims and causing them to feel extremely alone. As illness lingers, patients often experience a kind of "tunneling" phenomenon wherein they back into an emotional tunnel. They lose interest in world affairs, local news, and finally, if the sickness is of long duration, their interests may be confined to their room and bed.

Hospitalized patients are often surprised by the number of friends who remember them during their confinement. Several have exclaimed to me that they didn't realize they had so many friends.

A person who comes to such a patient in the name of "friend" can sometimes help the patient feel a little less lonely. The patient can be made aware that somebody cares.

A friendly visit from a person who cares can also serve as a reminder to the patient of the eternal Friend, the One who declared, "I have called you friends" (John 15:15). The Lord of heaven, the Friend of man! This truth is difficult for finite people to grasp. Yet what a comforting, life-transforming thought—to be on an intimate friendship basis with our Maker and Redeemer.

The poet Elizabeth Barrett Browning once asked a Christian acquaintance, "What is the secret of your life? Tell me, that I may make mine beautiful, too." The gentleman's answer was, "I have a Friend"—meaning Jesus.

No life is so dull or drab that it cannot be brightened by him. No soul, however ugly with sin, is beyond his pardoning grace and transforming friendship. He laid down his life for our redemption, and "Greater love has no man than this" (John 15:13).

"Thanks" Deserved

Not many people really know much about the life of a physician. Doctors are known by most people professionally, not personally.

There is little awareness of the long years of laborious study and enormous expenses necessary to become a qualified physician. Nor is the average person knowledgeable about the rigors of specialization or the costly task of furnishing and equipping an office.

The decisions doctors have to make daily and the life-or-death responsibilities that become their burdens would scare most mortals sleepless and useless. Yet the physician has to carry on with his own life in the face of these pressures.

His hectic schedule is interrupted twenty or thirty times daily by phone calls, some of which bring him information of emergency situations which must be dealt with immediately. Always there are the decisions to be made involving overwhelming responsibility.

The doctor's family and social life, as well as his sleep, is at the mercy of the health needs of others. A night filled with emergencies of auto wrecks, births, and broken bones will usually be followed by a day of previously scheduled appointments.

Neither has the doctor finished with his study when he is awarded the M.D. degree. His education has apparently only begun with so many new drugs and so much new equipment coming regularly into use.

Still, many people seem to take their doctors for granted. They seldom realize the sacrifices he may have made to be present with them during their time of need, for he never mentions those sacrifices.

A word of sincere appreciation to your faithful physician is probably in order. Perhaps he has not been "thanked" as often as one might imagine, and he certainly deserves it. "Only Luke [the physician] is with me" (2 Tim. 4:11, KJV).

Recovery

Jesus once asked a man who had been sick for thirty-eight years a most unusual question: "Do you want to be healed?" (John 5:6). The man's answer was ambiguous, not a clear-cut yes but a complaint: "I have no man to put me into the pool" (v. 7).

This man apparently didn't recognize the divine power in Jesus. He asked only that he help him into the "magical" waters of the pool of Bethesda. Jesus made no use of the local cure, nor did he comment on it.

It's interesting that the man had no one to help him, but maybe after thirty-eight years his family had died or dispersed. Maybe his complaints had driven them away.

But Jesus' question was fair. Did the man really want to get well? After all this time, could he face normal life? Some people find so many secondary gains in illness that they won't give up their illnesses.

Jesus healed him. Yet there is no mention of his praising God or following Jesus. When he was questioned in the Temple, he didn't know who had healed him.

Jesus found him in the Temple and said to him, "Sin no more, that nothing worse befall you." Strange! What evil could a man do while flat on his back for thirty-eight years?

Perhaps it was not what he had done; it was what he was. It was not the withered limbs so much as his withered spirit that endangered his life.

But the story didn't end there. Jesus said, "My father is working still, and I am working" (v. 16). They are still working with the withered spirits of the ungrateful and the unknowing. They are still working on those whose bodies are easily cured, but whose spirits are more difficult to cure.

Interpreting Illness

Nobody really plans to become sick. Yet, counting common colds and stomach and intestinal upsets, the average person has ten or twelve illnesses yearly.

There are four broad types of causal factors in illness: (1) defective organs; (2) invasions of bacteria, poisons, or viruses; (3) distortions caused by a life-style of too much of this (calories, work) or too little of that (vitamins, rest); and (4) accidents. A person overtaken by any one of these is forced to take time to recover, adjust, or succumb.

When Job's wife saw his suffering and the tragedy which befell him, she made a statement which in Hebrew has two meanings. It may be translated into English as either "Bless God and die," or "Curse God, and die" (Job 2:9). This is very interesting since it is actually our interpretation of a situation which can make it either a blessing or a curse.

The entire Book of Job considers the interpretation of illness. One Bible commentary states that the Book of Job aims not at solving the entire problem of suffering but at vindicating God and the latent worth of human nature against certain conclusions drawn from a partial observation of life.

Harry Emerson Fosdick, who is well known for his writing and for his forty years as pastor of the Riverside Church in New York, had a "nervous breakdown" when he was twenty-three. He called it "the most hideous experience" of his life. Later he wrote, "Without that experience I do not think I would have written one of my early books, *The Meaning of Prayer*." This book was Fosdick's attempt to interpret his illness. It has been translated into at least seventeen foreign languages and has been of immense help to many.

Wrestling with Illness

"And Jacob was left alone; and a man wrestled with him until the breaking of day. When the man saw that he did not prevail against Jacob, he touched the hollow of his thigh; and Jacob's thigh was put out of joint as he wrestled with him" (Gen. 32:24-26). "And there he blessed him. So Jacob called the name of the place Peniel, saying, 'For I have seen God face to face, and yet my life is preserved.' The sun rose upon him [he was] limping because of his thigh" (vv. 29-31).

This story seems to suggest some of the major concerns of the sick. Like Jacob, the patient must find appropriate approaches of dealing with aloneness, wrestling, limping, and blessing.

First, there is the issue of aloneness. Jacob's family and his possessions had all been left on the other side of the stream as he waited for an uncertain tomorrow. Hospitalization separates the patient from those he loves.

Like Jacob, patients seem to be wrestling with the unknown. Perhaps most importantly, they wrestle with anger—struggling for control of that feeling. They are away from the people and activities they love most. They are forced into dependency on others. Unanswerable questions about their illness frustrate them. No wonder they wrestle with anger.

Many patients will leave the hospital limping. No patient is fully healthy when he completes his period of confinement. The patient's limp will often point him beyond himself to a healing which is not limited by brokenness of body and is valid for all conditions of men.

Even amid all these barriers, there can be a blessing. Jacob's blessing was not easily won; not many genuine blessings really are. They often come after the "holding close and not letting go" until the morning breaks.

The Lady with the Lamp

Years ago in England there was a girl who looked much like an ugly duckling, but whose mother wanted her to become a social butterfly. In opposition to her mother's plans, little Florence grew up determined to become a nurse. Somehow she managed to receive special training, usually against everybody's wishes.

At that time England was at war. Every day thousands of wounded English soldiers were pouring into the hospital in the Crimea. They lay neglected with no one doing anything prop-

erly for them. Florence Nightingale tore through endless opposition in Great Britain and endless red tape in the Crimea to
establish order and decent care for the wounded soldiers. She
shared her woman's tenderness with the thousands of wounded
men. When they would call out in the night, she came to them
so faithfully with her lamp that they began to call her "The Lady
with the Lamp."

Her lamp became a symbol for all nurses. Her courage was a
challenge to all nurses—to be a person ready to serve, equal to
any emergency, carrying the cross of Christ through tremendous
difficulties. Florence Nightingale allowed her light to shine that
others might know the Light of the world.

The Origin of Hospitals

Though the fact is rarely recognized, hospitals were *not* first
created by the church. They were known in much earlier days in
the older civilizations of Babylonia, Egypt, Greece, and Rome.

The Grecian temples of Aesculapius were the first hospitals.
In Ireland a hospital was opened in 300 BC, and in India one was
begun in 252 BC. In Mexico one is known to have flourished
before Columbus.

These first hospitals depended for their support upon the pity
of mankind. The whole spirit of antiquity toward sickness and
misfortune was one of expediency rather than compassion. The
upkeep of hospitals was first taught as a duty when the implica-
tions of Christianity were perceived.

The word *hospital* first referred to the institutions where
hospitality was given to pilgrims en route to the Holy Land.
Many became so tired or ill through the rigors of the journey
that they had to stay for long periods. Some were so infirm that
they remained until their pilgrim friends called for them on the
trip back home. These older or infirm folk stayed at annexes to

the hospitals called "infirmaries." It is only since the turn of the century that the image of the hospital began to change for some people from a final stopping place where patients die to a place of healing.

Even though the first hospitals were not established by the church, it is clear that the church has certainly started many hospitals. There are hundreds of denominationally related hospitals in our country today.

Opening hospitals is a service the church has performed for many centuries around the world. The most difficult days in the history of any hospital occur before the doors are opened and the first patient is admitted. After that, in modern times at least, a hospital usually becomes self-sustaining.

While the church did not create hospitals, it certainly has originated more of them than any other organization. The church has always cared about the sick and has done much to provide for adequately meeting their needs.

The Spirit of a Hospital

You can feel a certain atmosphere in a hospital. Patients speak of it frequently, and many of them try to figure out what it is. It is a kind of mood or air of concern which is unique to hospitals.

One time I set out to determine its origin. The more I listened and observed, the more I realized that this spirit came from the people who work in hospitals. These individuals usually have a strong sense of dedication to their work. Their hours are long and hard. Patients don't stop needing their care at night and on weekends, so the employees' week is quite irregular. Special training is required, yet the employees' pay is moderate. I firmly believe that hospital employees are caring individuals who have dedicated themselves to help heal humanity's hurt.

Most patients add to the atmosphere of goodwill in a hospital by being thankful for the care they receive and complimentary to those who give it. In fact, many patients go out of their way to express their appreciation by giving candy, sending "thank-you notes," or even returning to the hospital after they have recovered to express their gratitude personally.

Some patients gripe and complain, but those who work in hospitals don't seem to let these patients' attitudes dampen their spirits. As a matter of fact, hospital workers understand that many people are hostile when they hurt. They take each patient's complaints seriously and try to correct problems, but they manage not to take criticisms so personally that they walk around with hurt feelings.

I am thankful for the Christian spirit of concern which has permeated the attitudes of the personnel who work in hospitals. My prayer is that hospital personnel will continue to work and serve in a manner which respects patients as persons whom God has created and for whom Christ died. Hospital personnel, also being such persons themselves, know how to deal with others with care. "Whoever gives to one of these . . . even a cup of cold water because he is a disciple, truly, I say to you, he shall not lose his reward" (Matt. 10:42).

The New Year

The new year has much to offer each of us, furnishing us an opportunity to begin again. A good track coach knows that many races are won or lost at the starting block. Many a runner knows at the end of a race that he would have made a better showing if he had gotten off to a better start. In the next year of our Lord, we have a chance to fulfill individually the wish of the poet Louise Fletcher (Tarkington) who wrote:

> I wish there were some wonderful place,
> Called the Land of Beginning Again;

Where all our mistakes and all our heartaches
   And all of our poor selfish grief
Could be dropped like a shabby old coat at the door,
   And never be put on again.

The new year offers us *a chance to forget*. Many things that happened in the past year should be forgotten. Worrying and brooding over past mistakes and unfulfilled goals would probably not motivate us so much as it would slow us down. The track star runs better without his warm-up clothes. Our past burdens are also best laid aside through the assistance of God's forgiveness.

The new year also offers us *an occasion to remember.* The ability to remember our good times gives us satisfaction. Even as past victories impel the runner to try to win again, our past successes move us on toward others. Our accumulated experiences (combined with our heredity) have made us what we are. The more we can learn from them, the more able we are to meet the beckoning, challenging future.

Actually, time measurements are arbitrary. We have devised ways of measuring time into years. The time involved in the new year will be no different than it ever was. The difference is within our thought concepts, but that is difference enough.

The new year affords us the opportunity to invest ourselves in the kind of good life which will draw eternal dividends. As we recognize and revere our Maker and as we respect and relate to our fellowman, we are making investments which will draw eternal dividends.

May the new year be for each of us:
   The freer step, the fuller breath,
     The wide horizon's grander view;
   The sense of life that knows no death,
     The life that maketh all things new.

—AUTHOR UNKNOWN

Easter

Easter is the season of the year when rabbits begin to receive credit for what chickens have been doing all year long. It is a time of new hats, Easter eggs, chocolate rabbits, and all the other symbols. However, Easter means more than this to many people, for it is also a time of renewed faith and church attendance. It is a season when many forget the temporal and, at least for a time, contemplate the eternal.

I remember when my grandfather announced proudly to our family that he had bought some new chickens which would lay colored eggs for Easter. I told my wife after we left that some "city slicker" had finally gotten to Grandpa. I could not believe that any chicken could lay colored Easter eggs. Yet when we visited in his home again just prior to Easter, he presented to our children one dozen eggs "naturally" colored in pale shades of green, orange, and blue.

This incident reminded me again that Easter is a time of belief, even in those concepts which are not completely understandable. I did not believe that hens could lay colored eggs, even though my grandfather told me that this was true. Now that I've seen it, I have to believe it.

I do not understand how Jesus Christ was raised from the dead, but others who saw it have told others . . . who have in turn told me, and now I believe. So Easter is a time when we should affirm or reaffirm our belief and faith in God's power over us in life or in death.

Freedom

July the Fourth for all Americans and August the Fourth for Afro-Americans are the two dates set aside each year for the celebration of the independence and freedom won for us by our forefathers. The signing of the Declaration of Independence and the Emancipation Proclamation are evidence that America is a land in which there is freedom for all.

Certain nations and peoples have demonstrated a genius for certain things. In ancient Greece citizens were educated in the arts and philosophy. The Romans had an aptitude for organization, government by law, and military might. The Hebrew people made their outstanding contribution through their genius for religion. Americans have shown ability in industry, free enterprise, and the use of vast material resources, but America first distinguished herself among the nations by her genius for freedom.

Today, however, freedom may be in dire danger. Our forefathers fought for it, and we must not take it for granted. Several perils threaten the freedom for which our country has always been proud. *Ignorance* is a danger to freedom because illiteracy among the masses prevents them from knowing the true facts, figures, and benefits of freedom. *Intolerance* is an enemy of freedom because love and brotherly kindness are vital ingredients of freedom. *Indifference* allows freedom to be taken away. It lives on freedom but, like a leech, gives nothing to it. *Intemperance* robs freedom of its meaning by attacking it at its very heart.

Is there anything which will ensure long life for freedom? Yes, there is! It is the practical and personal application of the Ten Commandments, the Golden Rule, faith, hope, and love. Wherever any people struggle and sacrifice for freedom they struggle with God's approval, if in the end the freedom is to be used for the good of humanity.

Is true freedom but to break
Fetters for our own dear sake,
And, with leathern hearts forget
That we owe mankind a debt?

No! True freedom is to share
All the chains our brothers wear;
And, with heart and hand to be
Earnest to make others free.

—AUTHOR UNKNOWN

Thanksgiving or Thankstaking?

Gratitude is an emotion to be felt and expressed to others. Some people enjoy giving or expressing their heartfelt thanks while some prefer always to receive the "thank yous" or praise. All of us manifest a need to be noticed, recognized, and praised.

Some express their gratitude for more devious reasons. Some people try to "butter up" everybody by constantly praising their every activity. This is one "technique" for making friends or for making people feel that they owe something in return for thanksgiving. Others give thanks out of a sense of duty. They thank parents or teachers, or even God, because they have been taught to do so for politeness or because it is that season of the year.

Some of us enjoy being thankful while others are almost embarrassed by it. On his television program Jack Parr once remarked to Billy Graham about the fact that ministers never receive applause. This seemed somewhat tragic to Jack, but Billy had not even thought about it. As a matter of fact, we English-speaking people may seem a little peculiar to the rest of the world in the area of giving and receiving thanks. We are among the few cultures which feel a need to have sufficient words to express the thought: "you are welcome." We repeat this phrase without fail in response to being thanked lest we be outdone. To thank a person for thanking us seems unnecessary for the rest of the world and almost irksome.

Of course, we set aside a season in our land to remind us not to forget thankfulness to God. And, certainly, we often overlook God's blessings and take them for granted.

But how should we thank God? We can learn to do this properly in our relationships with our fellowmen. We want to thank God truthfully and honestly, not because we have to or because we hope to obligate the Divine to do us some favor, but simply because we feel thankful toward him. And remember, "It is more blessed to give than to receive" (Acts 20:35).

Christmas Carols

A carol is a hymn of joy which announces the good news of the birth of Christ. The late, well-known evangelist J. Wilbur Chapman used to remark that where one person comes to believe in Christ because of the star, at least ten believe because of Christmas carols.

Take, for example, the hymn, "O Little Town of Bethlehem." It is sort of a call to Christmas worship. After a bloody war, Phillips Brooks rode from Jerusalem to Bethlehem on Christmas Day in 1865. Four years later—at the request of the organist, Lewis H. Redner, who composed the music—Brooks wrote one of the simplest of our Christmas hymns. He wrote it for boys and girls, but it has captured the hearts of adults as well. In the four stanzas of the hymn, we sing about (1) the place where Christ was born, (2) the way that he was born, (3) the prayer for him to be born, and (4) the hearts where Christ is born.

O little Town of Bethlehem,
How still we see thee lie!
Above thy deep and dreamless sleep
The silent stars go by;
Yet in thy dark streets shineth
The everlasting Light;
The hopes and fears of all the years
Are met in thee tonight.

For Christ is born of Mary;
And gathered all above,
While mortals sleep, the angels keep
Their watch of wond'ring love.
O morning stars, together
Proclaim the holy birth,
And praises sing to God the King,
And peace to men on earth.

How silently, how silently
The wondrous gift is giv'n!
So God imparts to human hearts
The blessings of his heav'n.
No ear may hear his coming;
But in this world of sin,
Where meek souls will receive him, still
The dear Christ enters in.

O holy Child of Bethlehem!
Descend to us, we pray;
Cast out our sin, and enter in,
Be born in us today!
We hear the Christmas angels
The great glad tidings tell;
O come to us, abide with us,
Our Lord Immanuel!

May each of your Christmas seasons be as joyful as a Christmas carol!

The Spirit of Christmas

The Christmas season does something to people. It raises the spirits of most people. Almost everyone is aware of the "Christmas spirit," and most people are influenced by it. This special attitude during the Christmas season is characterized in several ways.

Christmas is a time of *praising*. People who seldom ever sing will find themselves entering into "caroling" or humming or whistling some seasonal tune. It is a season when we don't worry quite so much about what the world is coming to, but rejoice more about Who has come to the world, namely the Lord Jesus Christ!

Christmas is a season of *giving*. We send cards and gifts to those who mean the most to us. This custom follows the example of the first Christmas when the greatest of all gifts was given: God gave his Son. Perhaps the best gift that we have to offer during the Christmas season is the gift of ourselves to God in service to mankind.

Christmas is also an occasion for *receiving*. We receive gifts and best wishes from our family and friends. We can also receive God's gift; we can make sure that there is room for Christ in our hearts and lives.

Christmas is a time of *forgiving*. The seasonal spirit encourages us to go ahead and send the card or gift to the friend or family member who has wronged us. A few typical "Scrooges" are usually won over by the Christmas spirit each year. God is also ready at Christmas time (or at any time of the year) to forgive those of us who have wronged him.

However, Christmas is not a joyous season for everyone. For some it serves as an annual reminder of the death of a loved one or of some tragic event. Others have a personal war going on within themselves and have no energy left with which to celebrate. The joy of others depresses them even more. Perhaps we can be of help to these who have "winter but no Christmas" by making ourselves and our understanding available to them in the spirit of the one who said that he "came not to be ministered unto, but to minister" (Matt. 20:28, KJV).

Work and Worship

According to the Scriptures, God never rests, that is, he never rests completely. He always continues to be active as Maintainer, Sustainer, and Superintendent of his creation.

Yet on one occasion Jesus was condemned for working. In the fifth chapter of the Gospel according to John, he was criticized for healing a man on the sabbath day. But this incident indicates that the Great Physician remains "on call" twenty-four hours a day, seven days a week.

No, God never rests. For that we can be grateful. How could Jesus' critics possibly have thought they were serving God when a sick man lay nearby who was in need of God's mercy? Jesus' action on that occasion had the effect of saying: Work and worship are not mutually exclusive. Rather, work becomes worship when two conditions are met: (1) when it is the kind of work God does, and (2) when it is the kind of work which meets the needs of men.

When Christian people perform the work of the Lord, their actions combine worship and work. When people see in their vocations opportunities to serve God by living and speaking appropriately for him, their duties constitute work-worship. Thus, as Jesus taught, some work is worship, and some worship is work. The secular can become sacred, and the work of the Lord can be performed by people who dedicate themselves to God.

The Fear of Aging

Ours is a future-oriented and youth-dominated society. No one wants to get old. We invest vast sums in children but little in the elderly. Old age seems to frighten us to the point of denying to ourselves that it will ever happen to us.

The cosmetic manufacturers are having a "heyday" because many people will do anything or use anything to stave off the outward signs of age. It does seem to be true that one of the manifestations of old age most damaging to the psyche is the lessening of physical attractiveness.

It is not difficult to understand what it is about old age that scares us. At a recent Conference on Aging it was suggested that the most frequent problems among older persons were: (1) lack of adequate income, (2) inadequate housing, (3) poor health, (4) loneliness and isolation from their communities, and (5) increased leisuretime with a lack of meaningful activity to fill it. To this list might also be added the fear of becoming dependent on others and the knowledge of the closer proximity of death.

Yet 95 percent of the millions of people in our country who are over sixty-five are not in institutions but function at some level at home. Our current view of aging is poles apart from the attitude which prompted Robert Browning to write the following lines:

> Grow old along with me!
> The best is yet to be,
> The last of life, for which the first was made:
> Our times are in his hand
> Who saith, "A whole I planned,
> Youth shows but half; trust God: see all,
> nor be afraid!"

In earlier times generally, and in Eastern cultures currently, age and experience seem to be revered and equated with wisdom. We, too, want long life; yet the prospect of old age scares us. Could it be that, even more than longer life, we need meaningful life? In our youth we can use activity to wipe the questions of value and meaninglessness from our thinking. However, we may fear that in our old age we will no longer be able to evade such questions as the meaning of life and death.

Christian faith is helpful at this point. Jesus promised to help us find both the truth which makes us free and the abundant life.

Time and the Father

Time is a "father" concept in the sense that we use the terms *Father Time* and *Grandfather Clocks.* Our Heavenly Father limited us to time; we are bound to it and governed by it. Our humanity and equality are often made clear to us when we realize anew that each person has only twenty-four hours in a day. However, we sometimes rebel against our finiteness by procrastination.

Gulliver, in Jonathan Swift's story, looked at his watch so often that the Lilliputians thought it was his god. Primitive people did not seem to be so time conscious as we moderns. Perhaps we Americans are the most time oriented of all peoples.

The tension between today and tomorrow sometimes frightens us, for we contemplate too many tomorrows. We imagine the financial reverses, illnesses, and accidents that the tomorrows might bring. Our energies become divided between the processes of living now and fearing tomorrow.

In such a situation we become spiritual orphans. We forget that we have a Father who cares. His grace is promised for the needs of today: "My grace is sufficient for you" (2 Cor. 12:9). But this grace is similar to the manna of the Old Testament: It cannot be hoarded, stored, quick-frozen, or banked. It must be used now. We cannot save it for tomorrow. But saving this grace is not necessary for, like the manna, God's grace will be available tomorrow as well as today.

Late Starters

Adults are often as blind to their real abilities as adolescents. Many people have not yet discovered all their talents. However, there are a few classic examples of people who eventually turned out to be remarkable producers.

Among them was a boy from New Jersey whose teacher suggested remedial education because he was inattentive, indolent, and "addled." His name was Thomas Alva Edison.

Then there was the French lad who had his parents wringing their hands. All he ever wanted to do was go fishing. His name: Louis Pasteur.

And there was the case of the little German "Dummkopf." He didn't speak until he was past three, and his parents were seriously worried about his stupidity. At twenty he began work in a grubby little office, wasting a lot of time doodling with mathematics. At thirty his doodles began to make sense to the scientific world. Little "Dummkopf's" name? Albert Einstein.

A farm boy from the Midwest was turned down by West Point, worked as a soda jerk, did a little better at a bottling works, and became part owner of a haberdashery store. Name? Harry S Truman.

Then, there were others who blossomed along the way in life. Take writers, for instance. Some, like Edgar Allan Poe, Edna St. Vincent Millay, and Francoise Sagan, made their names famous in their teens. Many more, like Stephen Crane, Truman Capote, and William Saroyan, became famous while still in their early twenties.

William Somerset Maugham was writing best-sellers in his late seventies. Goethe was past eighty when he completed *Faust,* and Thomas Hardy and George Bernard Shaw did some of their finest writing as they approached ninety.

Let us not despair. Maybe this will be the year when we will begin to make our major contribution in life.

Life's Punctuation Marks

Without punctuation marks, you could hardly read your newspaper. Punctuation marks resemble traffic signs. They tell the reader when to start, slow down, pause, or stop.

Life, too, has its punctuation marks. Consider the exclamation points which signal those big, exciting events: First day at school! First date! Marriage! A big promotion! The birth of a child!

Every life also has its commas, signals to slow down. They may take the form of illnesses, disappointments, closed doors, or changes of circumstance. Few people can go through life at top speed—they have to slow down for unexpected emergencies.

The most puzzling punctuation is the question mark. It indicates an unanswered problem. It signals the misfortunes we find hard to understand and harder to accept. Why am I so depressed? Why do I suffer? When will I get better?

One of the most persistent questions of all is, "Who am I, and what is my purpose for living?" "Why am I here, and what am I supposed to accomplish?" Actually, the "why" of our lives is far more important than the "how." Once we know why we are living, it doesn't matter too much how we have to live if we can accomplish our purposes. Once we find meaning, purpose, and significance, we can handle the "hows" more easily.

A full life includes all kinds of punctuation marks. We must try to understand and accept them all. For the Christian, every punctuation mark has meaning. "To everything there is a season, and a time to every purpose under heaven" (Eccl. 3:1, KJV).

Tell It Like It Is

We live in an advanced age of communication. Newspapers, magazines, books, pamphlets, radio, television, speeches, and sermons are constantly produced in an attempt to communicate. Yet, in spite of all these efforts, many people live in isolation and loneliness.

There are many problems in communicating when you consider the various shades of meaning that every word contains, the indefinite output of the human speaker, and the internally censored reception of the human ear.

Communication requires two components: sending and receiving. It is awfully difficult to keep on talking into a telephone without the conviction that someone, somewhere, is listening. It is equally difficult to keep on listening to a telephone if you are not convinced that someone is going to speak to you.

Yet we need to communicate. This need is often listed by psychologists as one of the basic urges or drives of human beings. Part of the enjoyment of a personal experience comes from relating it to others; and when our problems get us down, it brings us relief to share them with someone we trust.

When we try to lock our feelings and experiences inside, our bodies often "tell on us" through sickness. These ailments are caused by stress wrought within us by our noncommunication.

The psalmist said, "When I declared not my sin, my body wasted away" (32:3). However, a few verses later he said, "I acknowledged my sin to thee and . . . thou didst forgive" (v. 5).

Hands

"Whatever your hand finds to do, do it with your might" (Eccl. 9:10).

How revealing our hands can be. There are numerous ways in which they, even without words, express our feelings to others. We sometimes wring our hands in despair. Or we at times fold them quietly as though to say, "There is nothing more I can do." We have all been known to clench our fists in rage as though we wish to strike someone. Then there are those moments when we doodle our fingers in boredom. There are also those times when we extend our fingers and palms upward to ask someone for help.

Our hands can also help us express some positive attitudes toward others. Military people salute their superior officers. And we have a way of utilizing our hands to pledge our allegiance to our country. We often extend our hands in warm, friendly handshakes. We sometimes lift our hands in prayer. We offer our hands to help someone else and, in fact, often speak of this action in terms of "lending a hand." We can put our hands to work in some useful task for the good of others.

The Bible states that "the Lord's hand is not shortened, that it cannot save" (Isa. 59:1). Yet it is quite obvious that God characteristically uses our hands to get his work done. Perhaps you have already become acquainted with the familiar poem:

> Christ has no hands but our hands
> To do His work today;
> He has no feet but our feet
> To lead men in His way.

> —ANNIE JOHNSON FLINT

Let's put our hands to work for Christ and his church. Let's use our hands to serve others and glorify God in both our family and in our community. May the words of the old hymn be our prayer:

Take my life, and let it be
Consecrated, Lord, to thee;
Take my hands and let them move
At the impulse of thy love.

—FRANCES R. HAVERGAL

Do the Best You Can

In Europe there is an old, old clock on the tower of an ancient church. This clock is so old it was built in the days when clocks were given only one hand, the hour hand. All these years this clock has been doing the best it could with one hand. And people still look at it to check the correct time.

God challenges us to do the best we can with what we have, remaining who we are whatever the task. As we are able to accept our limitations as well as our challenges, we are facing the reality of our life situation squarely.

Every morning at 4:00 AM a young black man used to kneel down by his bed and ask God for guidance about what to do with his life. He first asked God to help him understand humanity, but God seemed to indicate that was too much to ask. So he began asking about animal life; but that also, God implied, was too difficult. Finally, he asked, "Tell me, then, about the peanut and the sweet potato." God seemed to answer that, while he could not tell him all about them, they were indeed more his size. Both his parents had been slaves. In 1862 his mother had first looked on his tiny black face in a miserable slave hut. She named him George. He himself later added Washington to make his name George Washington Carver.

Reconciliation

A student in clinical pastoral education, who was a seminary graduate and an experienced, ordained minister, had not visited his father for five years. The student had been deeply hurt by his parents' divorce when he was just a boy.

However, with the encouragement of his fellow CPE students, he decided to go visit his dad who was then a sick old man. After a sleepless night he went to see his father, taking his young son who had been a baby the only time his grandfather had ever seen him. The student's dad cried and embraced him; his stepmother wept. They welcomed him and his son into their home.

The student said later, "This was just the opposite of what I had expected. There was no anger or questions of why I hadn't been in touch, just joy over my coming to see them. I feel I can be a better father by being a better son, and I needed to be a son." The Bible teaches that "through God you are no longer a slave but a son, and if a son then an heir" (Gal. 4:7).

The Father—"a Kept Man"

There was a time when most fathers really were the heads of their families. They were not only the providers but also the ever-present decision makers. In rural life all the family members were the workers in the family businesses of farming, and the fathers were the business managers.

Nowadays the average father is often a kind of absentee family member. His work normally takes him away from home and often out of town. Sometimes he is actually around his family very seldom, even for meals. Also adding to the problem are the distractions of his social life and his tendency to hide from his family behind a newspaper or the television. Even at home he is often emotionally withdrawn from his family.

His wife and children soon learn not to depend on him for decisions. In time it occurs to such a father that he is being left out of family life. He feels like a "kept man," and he wonders why.

A father should kindly but assertively make his presence felt in his family. His children need to learn what a man is like. His sons want to learn how to be like him, and his daughters want to learn how to love someone like him.

Psychologists tell us that we have a tendency to identify our Heavenly Father with our earthly father. This places a tremendous responsibility on fathers. Are we fathers teaching our children that God is usually absent, withdrawn, or angry about being disturbed and that he doesn't really care about our needs or decisions?

Biblical fathers were appointed as priests for their families. Modern-day fathers can also guide their children in the way of the Lord. The father may not always be able to be a "resident father," but he can try to give of himself to his family when he is around, thus making a lasting contribution to family life.

Love and Sex

Today our problem with love and sex is not so much that of recognizing the physical reality of sex as it is one of restoring the psychological reality of love. Psychology has correctly emphasized the significance of sex in the capacity to love and has greatly contributed to the importance of sex education for happy marital living. But a popular misunderstanding accuses psychology of advocating sexual license. The contrary is true. Any competent psychologist knows that mature happiness involves the acceptance of limitations. Promiscuity is a neurotic stigma wherein sex is separated from love.

Christianity is accused of placing unrealistic restrictions on sex. Yet I find nowhere in the Bible the view that sex is sinful. The Scriptures do make a healthy effort to lift sex from mere animalism or body chemistry to the level of love.

The reality of human love is never fully experienced unless a person has belief in life or a belief in God's love for mankind. For support of this thesis, let me point you to those who write about love—the novelists and poets. When life has meaning for them, they write affirmatively of human love. When they are disillusioned about life, they write bitterly of love as if it were an obscene joke.

Consider Hemingway's two novels: *Farewell to Arms* and *For Whom the Bell Tolls*. The themes are identical: a hero and his beloved on the background of a military blunder. The first novel was written when everyone was disappointed with the failure of World War I. In this novel the girl dies, and the hero lives on in a desperate futility. The second novel was written at the beginning of World War II when we were hopeful of eventual peace. The hero dies, but the beloved lives on and hopes for a better world. In the first book love was treated as a mere physical act. But in the second book, Hemingway seems to say, "I never really believed in such a concept."

When we have confidence in life, love can be affirmed as being more than sex. The Bible is the best book for reviving our belief in life and love. The prophets compare the capacity of human love to God's love for his people. "For your Maker is your husband, . . . for the Lord has called you like a wife" (Isa. 54:5-6).

Food and Love

To an infant, food and love seem to go together. The baby's philosophy appears to be: "If you love me, feed me; and if you feed me, you must love me." I'm not sure that we ever outgrow that basic concept.

Pediatricians insist that babies be held and cuddled while they are being fed, no matter which method of feeding has been selected. Even as adults most of us enjoy our meals much more if they are taken in the presence of the family or friends. To eat alone is not an inviting idea to many people. Food continues to call for the appropriate surroundings of friendship and love.

In the patterns of living that most people in our country seem to have adopted today, mealtime is one of the few times when the family is together. This is only true for one or perhaps two meals per day. Yet this time is often a highlight of the day as family members share food, experiences, and love.

When married children visit their parents, a meal is often a part of that visit. More than one set of such older parents have complained that "the children and grandchildren came to visit us, but they didn't even stay long enough to eat." On the other hand, an adult who visits his or her parents briefly will often "want something to eat" even though not really hungry. Maybe he or she nibbles at a snack out of habit simply so they will feel like he or she has been home.

The Lord's Supper ought to be seen in a similar light. We gather around the Lord's table as equal siblings and are reminded of his love for us and our love for him. Does not the Scripture read, "Man shall not live by bread alone"?

Should We Seek God Individually
or with Others?

Psychologists tell us that one of mankind's basic needs is the gregarious need: the desire to be with people and to have communication with those of our own kind. This—along with the fulfillment of some other human needs such as the need for air, water, food, rest, and sleep—is considered necessary for survival.

We are all familiar with groups, and most of us enjoy being a part of them. We are born into a group, "the family." We are educated with a group, "the class." And we worship with a group, "the church."

In church circles, this is usually referred to as fellowship. Jesus seemed to be putting considerable emphasis on fellowship in Matthew 18:20: "For where two or three are gathered together in my name, there am I in the midst of them." Jesus promised to be in our midst even when only two or three of us gather in his name.

However, this verse of Scripture is not necessarily limited to church groups only. That couple who is pronounced man and wife in Jesus' name and realize the presence of a divine Third Party in their marriage is off to a good start. The pastor and parishioner who chat in Jesus' name may also be aware of the Third Presence. The chaplain and patient who converse are often aware of the divine Presence in their midst. A sense of the presence of the Almighty (which often gives the dialogue a prayerful atmosphere) is one of the factors which makes pastoral counseling unique. People everywhere may be assured that whenever they gather in Jesus' name to pray, talk, commune, work, confess, serve, or sing, Jesus is in their midst.

It is strange, in the light of this verse, that so many people have the idea that they can approach God best when they are alone. This verse indicates the importance and the power of the group. Perhaps we can best learn how God deals with us by relating to groups. As we allow ourselves to become better known by others in a group, we learn that even after other people come to know the bad about us, as well as the good, they can still respect us and befriend us—even love us. Then we can better understand how God can love us, even though he knows all about us. As we enlarge our capacity to know and love other people, we also enlarge our ability to know and love God.

When we relate to another person or persons in Jesus' name, we can be assured of his presence. He assured them: "All men will know that you are my disciples, if you have love for one another" (John 13:35).

Can You Believe It?

We Christians often sing a hymn beloved by thousands. This is the best-known stanza:

> Just as I am, without one plea,
> But that thy blood was shed for me,
> And that Thou bidd'st me come to thee,
> O Lamb of God, I come! I come!

My question is, "Do we really believe this?" I wonder if many of us do believe that God does actually love us as we are.

God does not love us *because* we are good. We do not earn his love. God does not love us *if* we serve him. We do not work for his love. God does not love us only *when* we do his will. We do not time God's love. Neither does God love us *so* we will be like he wants us to be. We are not manipulated by his love.

Yet, Scripture teaches that God does love us. He loves us because it is characteristic of him to do so. He is God, and "God is love" (1 John 4:8). God loves us because he wills to do so. It is often difficult for us to understand why he chooses to love so many who are so unlovely. Yet he does.

In the Old Testament there was a word set aside *(chesed)* which was used only to refer to God's loyal, steadfast, loving kindness toward persons. In the New Testament the Greek word *agape* was the word that was reserved to refer to God's love for his people. This divine love goes out to us without any demands or expectations toward those who receive it. We have a theological word to describe this concept. The word is *grace,* meaning unmerited favor. God is loving and gracious toward us because we are his creation.

Can we actually realize the fact that God loves us? Can we accept this love personally? I wonder.

Preparation for Blessings

The first time our family went camping, we barely got the tent up before it started raining. We huddled inside the droopy tent for family prayer time and then retired for the night. I had hastily chosen a poor location to stretch the tent. So, while most of the family slept, my wife and I worried about how our tent would weather the wind and rain as well as the water we could feel running under the floor.

If I had known as much about tent pitching as the ancient Bedouin-like Hebrews, we would have slept soundly and securely in a tightly stretched, well-ditched tent that night. They knew how to prepare for the blessing of a peaceful night of blissful sleep. Isaiah wrote, "Enlarge the place of your tent, . . . lengthen your cords and strengthen your stakes" (54:2).

I think God has a lot of both common and unusual blessings for us if we are willing to prepare ourselves adequately to receive them. If we have shoddily built our lives on shifting sand and have "pegged down" only a few loose stakes to believe in, there is little wonder why God has such a problem slipping us a blessing when a storm comes. However, if our lives are founded on the strong stakes of faith, hope, and love, and if our cords are lengthened in service to others, the blessings come.

God characteristically works so smoothly and quietly in our world and in our lives that only a few are perceptive enough to recognize his blessings. For instance, some have asked, "Why did God wait until Abraham was so old before he spoke to him?" Perhaps God was speaking all the time, but Abraham was seventy-five years old before he ever really listened to God.

We see what we look for. A big game hunter might go to Africa and see many lions but not even one missionary. Yet a missionary that I know lived in Africa for sixteen years and never saw even one lion.

Isaiah 54:2 was William Carey's text for his famous missionary sermon in which he made two points: Attempt great things for God and expect great things from God. If this Scripture passage could set in progress the modern missionary enterprise, then why can't we let it speak to us today?

God offers us his unconditional love. The question is: Are we ready to accept it?

After that first night of camping, our family stood and looked bewilderingly at the soggy, tottering tent. That day we moved it to a choice location, stretched it tightly, and were then really prepared to receive all the blessings of camping.

Prayer in a Crisis

In a time when we or our loved ones are in the midst of a crisis, most of us want desperately to pray. Yet we are sometimes like Saint Francis of Assisi, who used to sit in attempted prayer with no spoken word except the occasional exclamation, "God!"

For obscure reasons, we cannot speak or think or pray. We seem to be struck dumb by the awful rush of events which brought us into the emergency. Perhaps doubt or fear that "the worst may happen" assails our faith.

The words of relatives and friends help little, if any. Still we want to have these people present, if possible. We need the assurance which comes to us through their presence. Napoleon must have felt a similar need before his great battles when he reportedly stood in his tent while one by one the marshals and commanders of his armies entered, grasped his hand meaningfully in silence, then went out again.

Much can be learned in such an experience of crisis. This kind of learning through experience is difficult, yet possible. We must remember that genuine prayer is produced more through proper attitude than proper words. Thus, real and acceptable prayer is offered by the person in a crisis situation, even if a clergyman or friend has to supply the audible words. The apostle Paul climaxed a passage on prayer in Ephesians 6:10-18 in these words, "Pray at all times in the Spirit, with all prayer and supplication." This is probably just what happens with the person in a crisis who wants to pray.

How to Deal with Doubt

Don't be afraid to doubt. God can handle your questions. Elton Trueblood said, "If any . . . part of religion is not true, we ought to give it up."

Doubt your doubts. Many reject their childhood religion but try to replace it with a void. They reject the Bible but give credence to other books. They doubt the authority of Christ but accept the authority of men. They reject the testimony of Christian people but believe what other groups say.

Study and test your doubts. This is what Thomas did. He had little faith, but he could believe what he experienced personally. God honored that.

Discuss your doubts. Your pastor or a Christian friend can often help you.

Be patient with your doubts. Resolution may require a lot of thought and maturing.

Go beyond doubt to commitment. Dr. W. P. Faunce, one-time president of Brown University, used to tell his students that one must learn to question things "as the railroad employee tests the car wheels before the train starts out of the station. It is that man's doubt that ensures our safety in travel. But if we do nothing but test car wheels and never really dare to travel, our doubt has become irrational, paralyzing and preposterous." In short, doubt is all right as far as it goes, but it doesn't go far enough. As a famous clergyman once said, "Faith begins with an experiment and ends with an experience." Don't let your doubts keep you from the joyous experience that awaits every man who earnestly searches for God. In *The Pilgrim's Progress*, John Bunyan's famous allegory, Christian was imprisoned for a while in Doubting Castle, but his journey wasn't over until he reached the Celestial City!

Monument to a Misery

Too often our attempts to be thankful are limited to sighs of relief that we are "not as other men," in squalor or in sickness or in a Communist country. Yet, our problems are not always filtered out of our blessings.

The Christian has a different outlook than the humanitarian or the Marxist. To whom can the Communist give thanks, apart from himself or the ghostly memory of "Our Father Lenin"? We are not self-made men. Popeye, the sailor man, said in old cartoons, "I y'am what I y'am," but Paul, the apostle, said, "By the grace of God I am what I am" (1 Cor. 15:10).

In the town square of a village called Enterprise in southern

Alabama, the townspeople have erected a monument to an insect. It may be the only monument of its kind in the world. The monument honors the Mexican boll weevil.

In 1895 when this bug first appeared in Coffee County, the annual yield of thirty-five thousand bales of cotton was cut 40 percent. In desperation, the cotton farmers had to turn to more diversified farming. They began to raise potatoes and corn and, most of all, peanuts. By 1919 the country's peanut crop was yielding more than a million bushels annually.

During that year of prosperity, a fountain was built across from the courthouse square in Enterprise. The inscription reads:

> In profound appreciation
> of the Boll Weevil
> and what it has done
> as the herald of prosperity,
> this monument was erected
> by the citizens of
> Enterprise, Coffee County, Alabama.

This town has come to be known as the "Peanut Capital of the World." The citizens literally constructed a monument to a misery. Their difficult time of greatest adversity ushered in an era of great blessing.

The Case of the Cross Collector

There is a story about a pastor who was a cross collector. I do not mean that he was an angry acquirer. This minister simply had a hobby of collecting various models of the crosses which represent the wide range of traditions within Christianity. He had in his possession Saint Andrew's crosses, Maltese crosses, tau crosses, and many more.

However, on one occasion the cross collector did become an angry acquirer. It seems that he got crossed up. He eyed a cross of spikes on sale at England's Coventry Cathedral. This cross was alleged to have been fashioned from spikes used in the bombed-out cathedral. Having paid the price for his cross, he discovered the spikes were plastic fakes. It was a case of the cross-eyed double cross: cross cross collector.

There are a lot of people who have been carrying around fake crosses. These persons have allowed certain life events to weigh them down and have passed them off as their "crosses to bear." Yet it seems more scriptural to me to think of a burden as something thrust upon us whether we want it or not, while a cross is something that, like our Lord, we choose to carry because of its significance.

Some people choose no cross of any kind and grumble about their so-called burdens. They carry many such burdens that they need not carry at all. Bunyan in *The Pilgrim's Progress* rightly described Christian as the man who, when he met the Christ of the cross, felt his burden tumble off his back.

Others choose a variety of gaudy, multicolored phony crosses. When the flashing of these spectacular crosses brings rebuke or criticism from others rather than the hoped-for praise, they become confused. They should realize that they have been crossed off as merely cross collectors, not sincere Christians.

The *real* cross is concern for the spiritual welfare of other people. Jesus said, "He who does not take his cross and follow me is not worthy of me" (Matt. 10:38).

Acceptance of Death

There is something frightful about death for almost all of us. Yet the subject of death and dying has recently been given a lot of studious attention by psychiatrists, ministers, sociologists, and psychologists. They have suggested that a person usually passes through several stages as he moves knowingly toward death: shock and denial, depression, anger, hope, bargaining, grief, and acceptance. A question that is raised occasionally is whether or not death is always easier for a Christian. I would like to think it is, but my experiences as a hospital chaplain have taught me that this is not invariably true.

Death is sometimes easier for a Christian. This statement can be beautifully illustrated by the story of a lady in her fifties who had been a patient in the hospital for more than three months. A year prior to her admission she had told her pastor that she would like to be able to say the twenty-third Psalm at the time of her death and not be afraid. As her chance for recovery deteriorated, he began to quote it to her occasionally during his visits. On his last visit he asked if she would like for him to repeat "their Psalm." She smiled affirmatively. He took her hand in his and began to quote those familiar words. Just after he had said the phrase, "I will fear no evil," he felt her hand relax. A few minutes later the physician pronounced her dead.

I guess most of us wish for the kind of faith that would provide us with similar courage when our "time" comes.

Ask God Why

Dag Hammarskjöld was accidentally killed in an airplane crash while actively serving as presiding officer of the United Nations. Only one wreath of flowers was allowed on the grave at his funeral and on that wreath there was only one word: "WHY?"

I recall a patient who said, "I have tried never to ask God why." I also remember a minister whose wife was killed in an automobile accident. He, too, was injured in the accident and could not attend the funeral service. The minister who conducted the memorial service gave him a recording of the service. Nearly two years after his wife's death the minister said, "I have never asked God why." He still had the recording of the service but had never listened to it.

WHY NOT ASK GOD WHY? Are we afraid that God can't take it? Are we afraid that we may, with our questions, cause God to cease to exist? Or, are we afraid that our theology might crumble and wither away?

We do not by our assent let God be God. He is God. Nor can we with our questions or doubt or skepticism knock God out of his sovereignty. GOD IS GOD.

But we can be honest with God. We can admit to him our doubts and fears and anxieties in times of crisis. We can assure ourselves from God's Word that God loves us and that he is with us at all times. We urge our young people in college to ask questions, and some professors say that they can get some idea of a student's intelligence by the questions he asks. Why do we not think that we can learn in matters of religion by asking questions, even of God?

Perhaps if we will be more open with God and will take some of our questions honestly to him in prayer, we will get some answers. Maybe we can learn amid all the disappointments of life, the misunderstandings, and the unanswered questions that God is walking with us through all of life, that "God is our refuge and strength, a very present help in trouble" (Ps. 46:1).

Life or Death

A nurse called me to talk to a young mother whose baby was stillborn. The woman was deep in grief. She said that every time she had gone to sleep since her delivery, she had awakened herself screaming from bad dreams.

She confessed that when she had first become pregnant she did not want the baby because she already had other children. But during her pregnancy she had adjusted to the idea and had come to accept and desire the new baby. When it was born dead, she felt guilty and somehow responsible for its death.

The most therapeutic thing that I did was to quote a Scripture: "The Lord gave, and the Lord has taken away; blessed be the name of the Lord" (Job 1:21). I pointed out that she need not hold herself responsible for life and death. Such matters are too big for us mortals. These things are in the hands of God through the natural laws which he set in process long ago.

The next day when I entered her room, a Gideon New Testament was placed prominently near her bed. She pointed to it and said, "You know I couldn't read that Book until after our visit yesterday. But I've found some answers in it since then. And last night, I had my first good night's sleep since delivery!"

Part III

Poems
of Grace and Healing

The Eternal Goodness

And so beside the Silent Sea
    I wait the muffled oar;
No harm from Him can come to me
    On ocean or on shore.

I know not where His islands lift
    Their fronded palms in air;
I only know I cannot drift
    Beyond His love and care.
. . . .
And Thou, O Lord! by whom are seen
    Thy creatures as they be,
Forgive me if too close I lean
    My human heart on Thee!

—JOHN GREENLEAF WHITTIER

The Flurry-Go-Round

Come on, let's get off the Flurry-Go-Round,
The Hurry-Go-Round, the Scurry-Go-Round
The speed-driven, green-riven Worry-Go . . .
    The straining and blowing . . .
      And where are we going?

72

The cussing and fretting . . . and
    What are we getting?
The huffing and puffing, and
    Can't get enoughing,
The sweating and stewing . . .
    And what are we doing?
Just going around . . . and around . . . and around
Then what will we do with whatever we've
    Found
When we think that we're bound for six
    feet underground
When we finish our round on the Hurry-go-round,
While the Hurry-go-round goes around
    and around
And around . . . and around . . . and around.
    Do we have to fall off the Merry-Go-Round?
    Time will slap us all off the
        Merry-Go-Round.
    So why not crawl off the Scary-Go-
        Round
AND LET IT GO 'Round and Around and Around.
And Around, and Around, and Around!

—A COUNSELEE

Isolation

Quiet
Slow
Hospital Zone
Emergency Entrance
Surgery
No Visitors
Isolation

Intensive Care
Treatment in Progress
Visiting—Five Minutes per Hour
Visiting Hours: 2-4 PM
Quiet Please

—RICHARD DAYRINGER

O God, Our Help in Ages Past

O God, our help in ages past,
    Our hope for years to come,
Our shelter from the stormy blast,
    And our eternal home!

Under the shadow of thy throne
    Thy saints have dwelt secure;
Sufficient is thine arm alone,
    And our defense is sure.

Before the hills in order stood,
    Or earth received her frame,
From everlasting thou art God,
    To endless years the same.

A thousand ages in thy sight
    Are like an evening gone;
Short as the watch that ends the night
    Before the rising sun.

Time, like an everrolling stream,
    Bears all its sons away;
They fly, forgotten, as a dream
    Dies at the opening day.

O God, our help in ages past,
    Our hope for years to come,
Be thou our guard while life shall last,
    And our eternal home.

—ISAAC WATTS

No Coward Soul Is Mine

No coward soul is mine,
No trembler in the world's storm-troubled sphere;
    I see Heaven's glories shine,
And faith shines equal, arming me from fear.

O God within my breast,
Almighty, ever-present Deity!
    Life—that in me has rest,
As I—undying Life—have power in Thee!

Vain are the thousand creeds
That move men's hearts—unutterably vain;
    Worthless as withered weeds,
Or idlest froth amid the boundless main,

To waken doubt in one
Holding so fast by Thine infinity;
    So surely anchored on
The steadfast rock of immortality.

With wide-embracing love
Thy spirit animates eternal years,
    Pervades and broods above,
Changes, sustains, dissolves, creates, and rears.

Though earth and man were gone,
And suns and universes ceased to be,
    And Thou were left alone,
Every existence would exist in Thee.

    There is not room for Death,
Nor atom that his might could render void;
    Thou—Thou art Being and Breath,
And what Thou art may never be destroyed.

—EMILY BRONTË

Crossing the Bar

Sunset and evening star,
    And one clear call for me!
And may there be no moaning of the bar,
    When I put out to sea,

But such a tide as moving seems asleep,
    Too full for sound or foam,
When that which drew from out boundless deep
    Turns again home.

Twilight and evening bell,
    And after that the dark!
And may there be no sadness of farewell,
    When I embark;

For though from out our bourne of Time and Place
    The flood may bear me far,
I hope to see my Pilot face to face
    When I have crossed the bar.

—ALFRED, LORD TENNYSON

Consolation

Though he that, ever kind and true,
Kept stoutly step by step with you
Your whole long gusty lifetime through
   Be gone awhile before,
Be now a moment gone before,
Yet, doubt not, soon the seasons shall restore
    Your friend to you.

He has but turned a corner—still
He pushes on with right goodwill,
Thro' mire and marsh, by heugh and hill
   That self-same arduous way—
That self-same upland, hopeful way,
That you and he through many a doubtful day
    Attempted still.

He is not dead, this friend—not dead
But, in the path we mortals tread,
Got some few, trifling steps ahead
   And nearer to the end,
So that you, too, once past the bend,
Shall meet again, as face to face, this friend
    You fancy dead.

Push gaily on, strong heart! The while
You travel forward mile by mile,
He loiters with a backward smile
   Till you can overtake,
And strains his eyes, to search his wake,
Or whistling, as he sees you through the brake,
    Waits on a stile.

          —ROBERT LOUIS STEVENSON

Sonnet Thirty

When to the sessions of sweet silent thought
I summon up remembrance of things past,
I sigh the lack of many a thing I sought,
And with old woes new wail my dear time's waste;
Then can I drown an eye, unused to flow,
For precious friends hid in death's dateless night,
And weep afresh love's long since cancell'd woe,
And moan the expense of many a vanish'd sight:
Then can I grieve at grievances foregone,
And heavily from woe to woe tell o'er
The sad account of fore-bemoaned moan,
Which I now pay as if not paid before.
    But if the while I think on thee, dear friend,
    All losses are restored and sorrows end.

—WILLIAM SHAKESPEARE

Gifts

Have no fear for the gifts you give,
But the gifts you dare withhold—
In a world that needs your helping hand,
Your heart, your life, and your gold.

Death

Death, be not proud, though some have called thee
Mighty and dreadful, for thou art not so:
For those whom thou think'st thou dost overthrow
Die not, poor Death; nor yet canst thou kill me.

From rest and sleep, which but thy picture be,
Much pleasure; then from thee much more must flow;
And soonest our best men with thee do go—
Rest of their bones and souls' delivery!
Thou'rt slave to fate, chance, kings, and desperate men,
And dost with poison, war, and sickness dwell;
And poppy or charms can make us sleep as well
And better than thy stroke. Why swell'st thou then?
    One short sleep past, we wake eternally,
        And death shall be no more: Death, thou shalt die!

—JOHN DONNE

Hear him, ye deaf; his praise, ye dumb,
    Your loosened tongues employ;
Ye blind, behold your Saviour come;
    And leap, ye lame, for joy.

—CHARLES WESLEY

Standeth God Within the Shadow

New occasions teach new duties,
    Time makes ancient good uncouth;
They must upward still and onward
    Who would keep abreast with truth.
Tho the cause of evil prosper,
    Yet the truth alone is strong;
Tho her portion be the scaffold,
    And upon the throne be wrong:

Yet that scaffold sways the future,
    And, behind the dim unknown,
Standeth God within the shadow
    Keeping watch above his own.

—JAMES RUSSELL LOWELL

Thanatopsis

So live, that when thy summons comes to join
The innumerable caravan, which moves
To that mysterious realm, where each shall take
His chamber in the silent halls of death,
Thou go not, like the quarry-slave at night,
Scourged to his dungeon, but, sustained and soothed
By an unfaltering trust, approach thy grave
Like one who wraps the drapery of his couch
About him, and lies down to pleasant dreams.

—WILLIAM CULLEN BRYANT

The Nurse

To be a nurse is to walk with God,
Along the path that our master trod;
To soothe the achings of human pain;
To faithfully serve for little gain;
To lovingly do the kindly deed,
A cup of water to one in need;
A tender hand on a fevered brow,
A word of cheer to these living now;
To reach the soul through the body's woe,

Ah! this is the way that Jesus would go.
Oh, white-capped nurses in dresses of blue,
Our Great Physician is working through you.

—AUTHOR UNKNOWN

The Winner

Life's battles don't always go
    To the stronger or faster man;
But sooner or later the man who wins
    Is the fellow who thinks he can.

—AUTHOR UNKNOWN

Christina

Oh, we're sunk enough here, God knows!
    But not quite so sunk that moments,
Sure though seldom, are denied us,
    When the spirit's true endowments
Stand out plainly from its false ones,
    And apprise it if pursuing
Or the right way or the wrong way,
    To its triumph or undoing.

There are flashes struck from midnights,
    There are fire-flames noondays kindle,
Whereby piled-up honors perish,
    Whereby swollen ambitions dwindle.
While just this or that poor impulse,
    Which for once had play unstifled,
Seems the sole work of a lifetime
    That away the rest have trifled.

—ROBERT BROWNING

The Chambered Nautilus

Thanks for the heavenly message brought by thee,
    Child of the wandering sea,
    Cast from her lap, forlorn!
From thy dead lips a clearer note is born
Than ever Triton blew from wreathèd horn!
    While on mine ear it rings,
Through the deep caves of thought I hear a voice that sings:—

Build thee more stately mansions, O my soul,
    As the swift seasons roll!
    Leave thy low-vaulted past!
Let each new temple, nobler than the last,
Shut thee from heaven with a dome more vast,
    Till thou at length art free,
Leaving thine outgrown shell by life's unresting sea!

—OLIVER WENDELL HOLMES, M.D.

Almighty God of truth and love,
    To me thy power impart;
The burden from my soul remove,
    The hardness from my heart.
O may the least omission pain
    My reawakened soul,
And drive me to that grace again,
    Which makes the wounded whole.

—CHARLES WESLEY

The Celestial Surgeon

If I have faltered more or less
In my great task of happiness;
If I have moved among my race
And shown no glorious morning face;
If beams from happy human eyes
Have moved me not; if morning skies,
Books, and my food, and summer rain
Knocked on my sullen heart in vain—
Lord, thy most pointed pleasure take
And stab my spirit broad awake;
Or, Lord, if too obdurate I,
Choose thou, before that spirit die,
A piercing pain, a killing sin,
And to my dead heart run them in!

—ROBERT LOUIS STEVENSON

Lead, Kindly Light

Lead, kindly Light, amid the encircling gloom;
    Lead Thou me on!
The night is dark, and I am far from home;
    Lead Thou me on!
Keep Thou my feet; I do not ask to see
The distant scene; one step enough for me.

I was not ever thus, nor prayed that Thou
    Shouldst lead me on;
I loved to choose and see my path; but now
    Lead Thou me on!
I loved the garish day, and, spite of fears,
Pride ruled my will. Remember not past years!

So long Thy power hath blest me, sure it still
 Will lead me on
O'er moor and fen, o'er crag and torrent, till
 The night is gone,
And with the morn those angel faces smile,
Which I have loved long since, and lost awhile!

       —JOHN H. NEWMAN

The Ancient Mariner

In "The Rime of the Ancient Mariner" the poet Coleridge defined how many of us sometimes feel—
"Like one, that on a lonesome road
Doth walk in fear and dread,
And having once turned round walks on,
And turns no more his head;
Because he knows, a frightful fiend
Doth close behind him tread."

The ancient mariner knew loneliness when his fellow sailors died after the albatross was killed. Fortunately, his ship was carried to the shore of his homeland; but in order to cure himself of his loneliness and his guilt, the ancient mariner actually combined modern psychotherapy with ancient religion. He had to unburden himself by telling his tale to someone else. To do so, he restrained a man who was on his way to attend a religious function: a wedding. He told this stranger his troubles and then, rejoicing in the cure he had won for himself, he said:

O Wedding Guest! this soul hath been
Alone on a wide wide sea:
So lonely 'twas, that God himself
Scarce seeméd there to be.
O sweeter than the marriage-feast,
'Tis sweeter far to me,

To walk together in the kirk,
With a goodly company!—

To walk together to the kirk,
And all together pray,
While each to his great Father bends,
Old men, and babes, and living friends
And youths and maidens gay!

Farewell, farewell! but this I tell
To thee, thou Wedding-Guest!
He prayeth well, who loveth well
Both man and bird and beast.

He prayeth best, who loveth best
All things both great and small;
For the dear God who loveth us,
He made and loveth all.

—SAMUEL TAYLOR COLERIDGE

The Ageless Quest

Since remote in the past when Man became Man
Sound reason for the act has challenged his mind.
Deep in thought he has bemused the Plan
That filters through time to all his kind.

Cradled in caves and windswept terrain
Man yearned for the meaning through fire and stone.
Bewitched by the glories of firmament and grain
He turned to their worship awed and alone.

Spawned from fertile valley, mountain, and shore
Came a school of pagan idols in wondrous array.
Yet Man kept on yearning for something more
Than death and destruction to the end of his day.

Science and culture in the swift pace of time
Found him wise and discreet and proudly sound.
Shed of crude baseness, sophisticate sublime
He suddenly discovered the atom around.

But deep in the heart of today's bold soul
The thought still lingers—What of the Epistles?
Searching for the answer the doubter may toll
Only bells of neutrons and high flying missiles.

Deaf ears do not hear the call of the One
Who rose to a cross and up and beyond
For in Man's long quest to relate to the One
He chides the Holy Word and fails to respond.

'Tis true! 'Tis true! Like a bell ringing true.
The key to the Plan of the Master's hand
Is that Man from his God was split in two,
To be rejoined at last by the Savior's stand.

—ROBERT MAJOR MATHEWS, M.D.

To Make This Life Worthwhile

Make every soul that touches mine—
Be it the slightest contact—
Get therefrom some good;
Some little grace; one kindly thought;
One aspiration yet unfelt;
One bit of courage
For the darkening sky;
One gleam of faith
To brave the thickening ills of life;
One glimpse of brighter skies
Beyond the gathering mists—
To make this life worthwhile.

—GEORGE ELIOT

Forgiveness

My heart was heavy, for its trust had been
Abused, its kindness answered with foul wrong;
So, turning gloomily from my fellow-men
One summer Sabbath day I strolled among
The green mounds of the village burial-place;
Where, pondering how all human love and hate
Find one sad level; and how, soon or late,
Wronged and wrongdoer, each with meekened face,
And cold hands folded over a still heart,
Pass the green threshold of our common grave,
Whither all footsteps tend, whence none depart.
Awed for myself, and pitying my race,
Our common sorrow, like a mighty wave,
Swept all my pride away, and trembling I forgave!

—John Greenleaf Whittier

I Wandered Lonely as a Cloud

I wandered lonely as a cloud
    That floats on high o'er vales and hills,
When all at once I saw a crowd,
    A host, of golden daffodils;
Beside the lake, beneath the trees,
Fluttering and dancing in the breeze.

Continuous as the stars that shine
    And twinkle on the Milky Way,
They stretched in never-ending line
    Along the margin of a bay:

Ten thousand saw I at a glance,
Tossing their heads in sprightly dance.

The waves beside them danced; but they
    Out-did the sparkling waves in glee:
A poet could not but be gay,
    In such a jocund company:
I gazed—and gazed—but little thought
What wealth the show to me had brought:

For oft, when on my couch I lie
    In vacant or in pensive mood,
They flash upon that inward eye
    Which is the bliss of solitude;
And then my heart with pleasure fills,
And dances with the daffodils.

—WILLIAM WORDSWORTH

The King of Love

The King of love my Shepherd is,
    Whose goodness faileth never;
I nothing lack if I am His,
    And He is mine forever.

Where streams of living water flow
    My ransomed soul He leadeth,
And where the verdant pastures grow
    With food celestial feedeth.

Perverse and foolish oft I strayed,
    But yet in love He sought me,
And on His shoulder gently laid,
    And home rejoicing brought me.

In death's dark vale I fear no ill,
　　With Thee, dear Lord, beside me;
Thy rod and staff my comfort still,
　　Thy cross before to guide me.

Thou spread'st a table in my sight;
　　Thy unction grace bestoweth;
And oh, what transport of delight
　　From Thy pure chalice floweth.

And so, through all the length of day,
　　Thy goodness faileth never;
Good Shepherd, may I sing Thy praise
　　Within Thy house forever.

—HENRY W. BAKER

Hymn to God the Father

Wilt Thou forgive that sin where I begun,
　　Which is my sin, though it were done before?
Wilt Thou forgive that sin, through which I run,
　　And do run still: though still I do deplore?
　　　　When Thou hast done, Thou hast not done,
　　　　　For, I have more.

I have a sin of fear, that when I have spun
　　My last thread, I shall perish on the shore;
But swear by Thyself, that at my death Thy Son
　　Shall shine as He shines now, and heretofore;
　　　　And, having done that, Thou hast done,
　　　　　I fear no more.

—JOHN DONNE

On His Blindness

When I consider how my light is spent,
E're half my days, in this dark world and wide,
And that one Talent which is death to hide,
Lodg'd with me useless, though my Soul more bent
To serve therewith my Maker, and present
My true account, lest he returning chide,
Doth God exact day-labour, light deny'd,
I fondly ask; but patience, to prevent
That murmur, soon replies, "God doth not need
Either man's work or his own gifts, who best
Bear his mild yoke, they serve him best, his State
Is kingly. Thousands at his bidding speed,
And post o'er Land and Ocean without rest:
They also serve who only stand and wait.

—JOHN MILTON

Ode to a Skylark

We look before and after,
    And pine for what is not:
Our sincerest laughter
    With some pain is fraught;
Our sweetest songs are those that tell of saddest thought.

Yet if we could scorn
    Hate, and pride, and fear;
If we were things born
    Not to shed a tear,
I know not how thy joy we ever should come near.

—PERCY BYSSHE SHELLEY

To Sleep

A flock of sheep that leisurely pass by,
One after one; the sound of rain, and bees
Murmuring; the fall of rivers, winds and seas,
Smooth fields, white sheets of water, and pure sky;
I have thought of all by turns, and yet do lie
Sleepless! and soon the small birds' melodies
Must hear, first uttered from my orchard trees;
And the first cuckoo's melancholy cry.
Even thus last night, and two nights more, I lay,
And could not win thee, Sleep! by any stealth:
So do not let me wear to-night away:
Without Thee what is all the morning's wealth?
Come, blessed barrier between day and day,
Dear mother of fresh thoughts and joyous health!

—WILLIAM WORDSWORTH

Conscience

Methought I heard a voice cry, "Sleep no more!
Macbeth doth murder sleep!" the innocent sleep,
Sleep that knits up the ravell'd sleave of care,
The death of each day's life, sore labour's bath,
Balm of hurt minds, great nature's second course,
Chief nourisher in life's feast.

—WILLIAM SHAKESPEARE

Longing

Come to me in my dreams, and then
By day I shall be well again!
For then the night will more than pay
The hopeless longing of the day.

Come, as thou cam'st a thousand times,
A messenger from radiant climes,
And smile on thy new world, and be
As kind to others as to me!

Or, as thou never cam'st in sooth,
Come now, and let me dream it truth
And part my hair, and kiss my brow,
And say: *My love why sufferest thou?*

Come to me in my dreams, and then
By day I shall be well again!
For then the night will more than pay
The hopeless longing of the day.

—MATTHEW ARNOLD

To Sleep

O soft embalmer of the still midnight,
    Shutting, with careful fingers and benign,
Our gloom-pleas'd eyes, embower'd from the light,
    Enshaded in forgetfulness divine:
O soothest Sleep! if it so please thee, close,
    In midst of this mine hymn my willing eyes,
Or wait the "Amen," ere thy poppy throws
    Around my bed its lulling charities.

Then save me, or the passed day will shine
Upon my pillow, breeding many woes,—
  Save me from curious Conscience, that still lords
Its strength for darkness, burrowing like a mole;
  Turn the key deftly in the oiled wards,
And seal the hushed Casket of my Soul.

—JOHN KEATS

Now the Day Is Over

Now the day is over,
    Night is drawing nigh,
Shadows of the evening
    Steal across the sky.

Jesus, give the weary
    Calm and sweet repose;
With Thy tend'rest blessing
    May our eyelids close.

Grant to little children
    Visions bright of Thee;
Guard the sailors tossing
    On the deep blue sea.

Comfort every sufferer
    Watching late in pain;
Those who plan some evil,
    From their sin restrain.

Thro' the long night-watches,
    May Thine angels spread
Their white wings above me,
    Watching round my bed.

When the morning wakens,
    Then may I arise,
Pure and fresh and sinless
    In Thy holy eyes.

—SABINE BARING-GOULD

Hymn to the Night

I heard the trailing garments of the Night
    Sweep through her marble halls!
I saw her sable skirts all fringed with light
    From the celestial walls!

I felt her presence, by its spell of might,
    Stoop o'er me from above;
The calm, majestic presence of the Night,
    As of the one I love.

I heard the sounds of sorrow and delight,
    The manifold, soft chimes,
That fill the haunted chambers of the Night,
    Like some old poet's rhymes.

From the cool cisterns of the midnight air
    My spirit drank repose;
The fountain of perpetual peace flows there,—
    From those deep cisterns flows.

O holy Night! from thee I learn to bear
    What man has borne before!
Thou layest thy finger on the lips of Care
    And they complain no more.

Peace! Peace! Orestes-like I breathe this prayer!
　　Descend with broad-winged flight,
The welcome, the thrice-prayed for, the most fair,
　　The best-beloved Night!

—HENRY WADSWORTH LONGFELLOW

Church Notes

For the musicians:　varied symbols of sound and rhythm climbing the staff ladder which direct behavior;

For the preacher:　thought nudgers of ideas meant to be shared with everyone;

For the business manager:　negotiable commercial papers relating to the church's debt which only paper currency from many people can repay;

For lovers:　something personal, intimate, confidential, handwritten, tightly folded, and secretly passed to one special person;

For the pastoral counselor:　documented feelings, concepts, interactions, interpretations, locked away and seen by absolutely no one else.

—RICHARD DAYRINGER

Worship

Lord, what a change within us one short hour
Spent in Thy presence will avail to make!
What heavy burdens from our bosoms take,
What parched grounds refresh as with a shower!
We kneel, and all around us seems to lower;
We rise, and all, the distant and the near,
Stands forth in sunny outline brave and clear;
We kneel, how weak! we rise, how full of power!
Why, therefore, should we do ourselves this wrong,
Or others, that we are not always strong,
That we are ever overborne with care,
That we should ever weak or heartless be,
Anxious or troubled, when with us is prayer,
And joy and strength and courage are with Thee!

—ARCHBISHOP TRENCH

"physician"

your hands
created for the art of healing

deft touches
gentle prods

your motions firm
your fingers steady

i put my life
between those hands
trustingly i await
your palms

you shape my clay
with careful strokes
putting it back
into its rightful form

death is thwarted
my spirit sings

—NANCY SUE PISTORIUS

"infection"

i doze unaware while beneath my skin
germs creep like fingers down my spine
swim downstream through channels of blood
then multiply militarily

my body becomes a battleground
teeming with fierce alien soldiers
its outraged tissues marshal forces
rise up hotly in savage defense

antibodies swarm to meet the bacteria
with bright-eyed vigor they attack
slaying microbes with sharp-edged swords

the enemy offers grim resistance
fighting to the death in furious combat
but falling back at last in quiet defeat

i doze unaware while beneath my bones
countless brave warriors are rejoicing

—NANCY SUE PISTORIUS

"a season of darkness"

i shall survive this winter
my flesh will not wither
or flake away
my eyes shall remain firmly fixed
in their sockets
staring straight ahead
at the light beyond
my snow shall not
fall hurt
and bleeding

—NANCY SUE PISTORIUS

"time, the invisible mender"

give me your throbbing wounds
i heal
skillful and steady-fingered
i knit together the walls of your womb
i stitch up the fragments of your soul

give me your poor weary limbs
i soothe
restful and serene
i stroke away the soreness in your muscles
i ease the aching in your troubled heart

come to me for comfort
for relief from pain

my touch never trembles
my gaze never wavers

my liniment never burns
my bandages never bind
my injections never sting
my medicine never spoils

i am a noble physician
i cure all

—NANCY SUE PISTORIUS

"for william edward"

two years beautiful
he died
still a little child
he never knew
the pain
of defeat
he never knew malice
or hate
he never knew doubt
or fear
he only knew
love

he gave me
his smile
before he died
one small smile
so brave
so sweet
i gave him
only tears

my sorrow
would have puzzled him
for he never knew
grief
he never knew
death

but death knew him
chose him
watched him
waited for the chance
to pluck him
from his mother's arms

now those arms are
empty
the crib is gone
the mickey mouse toy
and tiny white shoes
are stored in a
musty box in the attic
and his body
lies in another little box
beneath a small tombstone

our baby sleeps
the sweet sleep
of innocence
of joy undefiled
the world can never
touch him
with its greedy, callous arms
for our baby
died
two years beautiful

—Nancy Sue Pistorius

R.R.HESTER

Part IV
Messages
of Reassurance

The Great Physician

There are several stories about the actions of Dr. Victor Frankl, a psychiatrist, during the days of World War II. As he was of Jewish descent, his life was in danger.

One day some of his good friends brought him a visa which would permit him to leave Germany and travel to America. To leave and come to America meant to live. To stay in Germany might well mean his death. Dr. Frankl thanked his friends very kindly for obtaining his visa. Nevertheless, he explained to them that he really could not make such a decision as this until he had what he chose to call a "hint from heaven."

He left his office that day (not having yet picked up his visa) and walked over to his parents' home. There he found his father sitting at the kitchen table examining a small piece of marble. He asked his father what he had. His father said that on his way home that day, he had stopped at the ruins of the Jewish synagogue that a Nazi bomb had blown to bits. He had dug around in the rubble and had found a piece of stone. It obviously was a piece from the marble tablet of the law that contained the Ten Commandments. Dr. Frankl asked his father if he could tell from which commandment it came. He said, "Oh, yes, it came from the one that says 'Honour thy father and thy mother: that thy days may be long upon the land which the Lord thy God giveth thee!'" Dr. Frankl had his "hint from heaven." On that basis he chose not to take the visa and travel to America but to stay in Germany. He was arrested, as were his parents and his wife and family. None of his family survived. He himself once weighed less than a hundred pounds in the German concentration camp, but he lived.

Luke, the physician, in writing his story about the life of Christ, never got very far away from the sensitive humanitarianism of a conscientious physician in writing his Gospel. He found people sick and in need of help. He pointed them to their supreme friend and Savior, the Great Physician. He who is the Great Physician said, as recorded in the fifth chapter of Luke's Gospel, "Those who are well have no need of a physician, but those who are sick" (v. 31). Jesus himself is sufficient. He is also Savior to those in deepest need.

Once in a worship service with my students in Clinical Pastoral Education, the group was asked to choose some biblical character that each person in the group reminded them of. The group decided that I reminded them of Luke. I considered that quite an honor. Paul called Luke the "beloved physician" (Col. 4:14). On another occasion, after others had left him, Paul said, "Luke alone is with me" (2 Tim. 4:11).

Jesus has often been called the Great Physician. He was the Great Physician when he walked on the earth, and he still is now. When we think of Jesus as the Great Physician, we often think about how he can help those whose situation is hopeless. The Great Physician is of a great deal of help to such people in relieving them of pain, in helping them to understand what is happening to them, and in helping them to accept the fact that God has created life in such a way that it honorably ends with death. The Great Physician may sometimes help the terminally ill by giving them a little longer to live than perhaps they had expected, by giving them more good days than they felt they could count on, or by helping their families to be able to face their dying as well as the patients so often do.

There are also some other ailments which may require the help of the Great Physician. Psychosomatic ailments, perhaps better termed "emotionally induced symptoms," make us ill and cause us to have pain and dysfunction. These ailments include such things as headaches, ulcers, or skin problems. It may be that the Great Physician is more able to help us with such problems than anyone else. Peace with God through the Great Physician may go as far as any medicine in relieving such ailments as these.

Some ailments certainly do require the aid of the Great Physician if ever we are to get over them. One of these disorders is spiritual snobbery. Some people think that sickness is a punishment sent from God. That's what Job's friends thought. Job became ill; and his friends, Eliphaz, Bildad, and Zophar, came to "comfort" him. That's what they said. What they actually did was to look down their noses at him because they felt that he had sinned and that was the reason that he was sick. Finally, Job said to these three, "Worthless physicians are you all." They accused him of sin and disobedience to God rather than listening to him and actually comforting him as they had said they came to do.

The Great Physician can help us with the spiritual disease of hypocrisy. Some of us pretend to be something that we are not. When Jesus visited his hometown of Nazareth the first time, he quoted a proverb. He said, "Physician, heal yourself." He felt that his friends in Nazareth wanted to say that to him. He had just read to them from the scroll of Isaiah about how the spirit of the Lord was upon him to heal the sick and to comfort the afflicted. They had a lot of difficulty recognizing Jesus as the Messiah. Yet he identified himself exactly as he was.

We are prone to convince ourselves that we have a great deal of knowledge, skill, and expertise which really is not ours. A physician who is a good friend of mine realized some years ago that he was not all he wished to be to patients, nor was he all that his patients expected him to be. He closed his office for a year, went to the Menninger Foundation, and there studied psychiatry and psychosomatic ailments. He tried to learn how to listen to his patients and understand them. Since that year of study, he now takes more time with each patient and is greatly appreciated for it.

Another spiritual ailment that the Great Physician can help with is guilt. King David, after committing the sin of adultery, wrote the Psalm 32, "When I declared not my sin, my body wasted away/through my groaning all day long./For day and night thy hand was heavy upon me;/my strength was dried up as by the heat of summer." The Great Physician is able to help us when guilt is hanging heavily over our heads. According to David and according to modern medicine as well, carrying around a great deal of guilt can actually make us sick and cause our bodies to dysfunction. When we confess our sin as David did, the Great Physician can enable us to experience forgiveness and feel good again.

One other ailment that the Great Physician is able to help us with is pride. Many of us build up a great deal of self-confidence in the things that we do. Others learn to depend upon God to do things throughout their life. The physician who delivered me into this world always took a little bit of time to be alone before he went into surgery. As a physician and a surgeon, he, of course, had delivered babies and performed all the various kinds of surgery dozens, scores, maybe hundreds of times. And yet those in the little county-seat town of Carthage, Missouri, where I was born, knew that he never delivered an infant or performed surgery without first bowing and spending a few moments in prayer. The Great Physician is able to help us to realize our need of his help, come what may.

I believe in divine healing. I believe that all healing is divine. God has given knowledge, ability, and capacity to physicians and nurses to treat, to use medication, and to set broken bones. Yet not a one of them can heal. God does the healing. God uses the skills and the knowledge that he has given these professionals to bring about healing. This situation depicted is quite well in the closing scene of the film entitled *The One Who Heals*, produced by the Department of Medicine and Religion of the American

Medical Association. In this scene, a physician and a minister
are talking together in the hospital about the kind of day that
they have had. In the background there is the picture of a
French physician, Dr. Ambrose Peré. The physician (as he
points to the picture behind him) states that he agrees with Dr.
Peré who said, "I treat. God heals."

Let me close with one more story from the life of Dr. Victor
Frankl. Dr. Frankl was arrested and taken with other Jewish
prisoners in a train boxcar to the Buchenwald concentration
camp. The prisoners were unloaded from the boxcar, and some
were pointed in one direction to go through a door. Others were
pointed in another direction to go through a different door. Dr.
Frankl only learned later that if he had been pushed through the
other door he would have gone to his immediate death. He went
through the door with those who were going to be allowed to
remain alive at least for a time. They entered a room, and there
they were told to disrobe and turn in their clothing.

Dr. Frankl, of course, had on warm clothing in preparation for
the German winter. In exchange for their clothing, they were
given tattered, torn, and threadbare clothing that had been
taken from the bodies of some prisoners who had not survived.
Dr. Frankl had only had time to take with him one thing when
he was arrested: his most prized possession, a book manuscript,
his brainchild and gift to the world. He had been able to grab up
that manuscript in a hasty moment and stick it down into the
deep pocket of his overcoat. He knew, though, that there was no
need to try to save it. He just left it in the pocket of the overcoat
as he took it off and then put on the ragged, threadbare clothing
of a former prisoner. He was dejected and depressed. He
wondered if he could ever recapture the words he had written.

In disgust, he thrust his hands down into the pockets of the
worn-out coat he had been given and was forced to walk outside
in the cold. As he walked along, he realized that there was a
piece of paper in that coat pocket, too, and in disgust he told

himself, "Well, this must be what I have traded my manuscript for." He fingered the little piece of paper for a while and finally decided he might as well take it out and see what he had traded for. He was later to decide that maybe the trade was not so bad after all.

What he found in that pocket was a page out of the Bible, a page from the Book of Deuteronomy which the Jewish people call "the Jewish Shema" (see Deut. 6:4 *ff.*). It began like this: "Hear, O Israel: The Lord our God is one Lord: And thou shalt love the Lord thy God with all thine heart." He hung onto that piece of paper. He kept it, and it kept him through the days of his imprisonment. He emerged from prison at the end of the war and since then has written several books that have been translated into several languages and have been of help to many, many people.

I have cited stories of several physicians because I think that these doctors have some of the characteristics of the Great Physician. I dare say that your own doctor may remind you in one way or another of the Great Physician, Jesus Christ, who is the Physician of all times.

Don't Give Up Hope

A middle aged lady lay in her bed, fighting to stay alive to see her daughter's wedding. She had been incurably ill for the previous five years, but somehow she had been inspired to fight against the ravages of her illness until such time as her daughter had grown up, met a young man, fallen in love with him, and planned to be married.

The fifth verse of Psalm 42 states,

Why are you cast down, O my soul?
    and why are you disquieted within me?

Hope in God; for I shall again praise him,
   my help and my God.

Hope is a strange little word that says much to a lot of people.
Yet it speaks to people in quite different ways. As I began to
think about this word, I looked into the *Encyclopedia Britannica*
and found several columns devoted to love and more columns to
faith, but hope, poor little hope. She was not even listed.

Hope can be deceptive and discouraging. I think we usually
overlook that aspect of the concept of hope. For instance, the
Greeks considered hope to be an evil. Aeschylus called it "the
food of exiles." Euripides said it was "man's curse." Zeus used
Pandora to inflict revenge on mankind. Curiosity led her to open
the now-famous box from which emerged all the evils of the
world. Hope remained behind in the box. Cowley called hope
"fortune's cheating lottery, where for one prize a hundred blanks
there be." And even Shelley, the poet, in his poem "The Cinci"
said, "Worse than despair, worse than the bitterness of death, is
hope." Nietzsche, the philosopher, in his book *Human All Too
Human* wrote that "Hope is the worst of evils, for it prolongs the
torment in man."

Hope has also been studied by a psychological experiment at
Johns Hopkins University where rats were placed in large vats of
water which seemed to permit no chance of escape. In this kind
of hopeless situation, even vigorous animals gave up rapidly and
succumbed to death. But when the hopeless feature was elimi-
nated, then a rat that would certainly have died in another
minute or two became active and aggressive, swimming vig-
orously for even as many as fifty or sixty hours.

Yet we usually think of hope in a positive way. Hope certainly
can be encouraging and inspirational. Paul, the apostle, was loyal
to his Hebrew heritage as it is presented in Psalm 42 and Isaiah
40 when he wrote in 1 Corinthians 13 that hope should stand
with faith and love. Martin Luther said, "Everything that is done
in the world is done by hope." Samuel Johnson, the English man

of letters, wrote, "Where there is no hope, there can be no endeavor." Emerson, our American poet, stated, "It is by his hope that we judge a man's wisdom." Reverend Sam Jones, the Methodist preacher, said, "You cannot put a great hope into a small soul." Alfred, Lord Tennyson wrote about "the mighty hopes that make us men."

Hope does something to human beings to encourage them to keep on striving even when others with less hope have given up. For example, in World War II physicians were treated just like the rest of the prisoners in the Buchenwald Prison Camp in Germany. They were awakened at 4:00 AM in the morning. They stood for a shivering roll call and then made the long march to the German *autobahns* where they worked from daylight until dark. Then they marched the long distance home again for another shivering roll call and finally a cold, thin bowl of soup at bedtime. They were starved, beaten, and overworked like the other prisoners with no reason to expect any other fate than the miserable death and cremation which they observed daily. But at night when the other prisoners were asleep the doctors huddled together in a group and talked. They formed themselves into a medical society and took as their task the improvement of the health conditions of the camp and the medical care of their fellow prisoners. They discussed cases and presented papers on medical subjects. They even smuggled in enough equipment to build a very primitive X-ray machine that actually worked. They accomplished all these things in their efforts to help their fellow prisoners. This illustrates what dedication to medicine and humanity can do, if kept alive by hope.

There is yet a third dimension to the concept of hope, and I would be remiss if I did not mention it. I am referring now to "Christian hope." This concept takes the Christian a little beyond the average hope of mankind. When I speak of the Christian hope, I mean the hope that somehow we can make the best out of our existence and learn to live the more abundant life that Christ promised us. We Christians are ordinary people who worship an extraordinary God. He loved us so much that he was willing to give his Son, Jesus Christ, as an example in order that we might be able to make the best out of our lives. When we think about Christian hope, we are also thinking about some hope beyond this life, some hope beyond death.

I would like to offer a personal observation about hope: adults appear to hope a great deal less than children. It is easy enough to observe the child who hopes for a new toy, the child who hopes to go swimming on Saturday, the child who hopes for a big Christmas, the child who hopes to get well when he or she is ill. It is easy enough to detect hope in the face of a child, but it is rare to find it among adults. Somehow as we grow up, we accept the realities of life but we lose, or at least temper, our idealism and hope. Renewed hope is one of the things that our children have to teach us.

Dr. O'Neal said in a Clinical Pastoral Education lecture in New Orleans, that clergy should make their own diagnoses. It is natural for the patient to accept the diagnosis that the physician gives. Yet a diagnosis with a poor prognosis usually snuffs out all recovery. Dr. O'Neal said that the thing that no physician can measure is the hope within the soul of the individual that may help him or her cling to life far longer than the physician has ever observed before.

My own sister-in-law is an excellent example. When she was in the hospital in 1966, her doctors told us they did not expect her to live more than six months to a year or, perhaps at the very most, two years. But she had two small boys whom she loved dearly and whom she wanted to see grow up. So she became one of the best, most compliant patients any doctor could ever hope for. She is still living today. One of her physicians told me that he knew that her Christian faith and hope certainly helped every bit as much as the medicine that she had taken. Don't give up hope, no matter who you are, no matter what your diagnosis, prognosis, or hope for recovery. Don't give up hope. It is one of the best things you have going for you.

True Happiness

In times of illness and confinement all of us have more time to think. The question of what brings happiness often occurs to us. Other questions spin off this one and haunt the sick. What is the greatest good in life? What is life all about anyway? How can I make my life worthwhile and get in on some of the happiness that others seem to be having?

This may be a new question for you, but it is, of course, an old, old question. It was first dealt with most seriously in writing in the Old Testament Book of Ecclesiastes in about 200 BC. The author was a philosopher who cataloged King Solomon's moods of pessimism, hedonism, sophism, and faith. Renan, the French historian, has called this book "the only charming book a Hebrew ever wrote." Clyde Francisco, an Old Testament scholar, wrote that it is "an essay on the highest good."

The writer seemed to have four worrisome, obsessional thoughts. First, he thought that "all is vanity." He said it over and over. Another of his ideas was that one might as well eat, drink, and be merry, and simply enjoy life for that may be all there is. Third, he felt that there was no progress in the world. He used the phrase that there is "nothing new under the sun" twenty-five times in his little book. His fourth conviction was that maybe death does end all things. These four ideas kept coming back to him like yo-yos, preying on his mind and influencing his life. Ecclesiastes is a record of Solomon's ideas about happiness and some of the ways he struggled to find it.

As a young man, growing up as a member of the royal family in the palace, Solomon thought that if he could ever become the king and succeed his father, David, on the throne, that certainly this event would bring him happiness.

Of course, the day came when he was crowned king. But following the coronation he began to know something of the responsibility that goes along with kingship. He found that the king is deluged with the opinions of powerful people and pressure groups who want him to make each decision in their favor. Pleasing his court, his subjects, himself, and God was not easy. Being king did not bring him genuine happiness.

Then Solomon began to think that if he could have the wisdom to rule his people well, he would certainly attain happiness. This is typical of many young people who feel that once they get enough answers to the world's questions that happiness will just sort of accompany knowledge. Yet many educated people are very unhappy and sometimes "intelligently devastated" by life.

Solomon has a dream in which God offered to grant him his wish for wisdom to rule his people well (1 Kings 3:5-9). God told him that since he had not asked for riches, revenge on his enemies, or long life that he would grant the wish. The wisdom of Solomon began to spread far and wide. He founded a school of wisdom that produced Ecclesiastes and much of the other Wisdom Literature of the Old Testament.

Yet his conclusion concerning wisdom is in verse 18 of Ecclesiastes 1: "For in much wisdom is much vexation, and he who increases knowledge increases sorrow." And furthermore, "Of making of many books there is no end, and much study is the weariness of the flesh" (Eccl. 12:12). He found that, even though he did become wise and ruled his people well, true happiness was not to be found in wisdom.

He wondered where else he might look for happiness, and he began to think that perhaps he could find it in pleasure or sensuality. He turned from wisdom to pleasure much as Goethe's Faust, who, having failed to solve life's riddles by study, plunged deep into the sensual delights that he might still the burning thirst of passionate desire.

King Solomon was much like Sören Kierkegaard, the Danish philosophical theologian. Kierkegaard tried for awhile to live what he called the esthetic life, which made enjoyment its principle, only to experience its radical failure which he so lucidly described in his book *Sickness Unto Death*: "In the bottomless ocean of pleasure, I have sounded in vain for a spot to cast anchor." He wrote in his Journal: "I have felt the most irresistible power with which one pleasure drags another after it, in the kind of adulterated enthusiasm which it is capable of producing, the boredom, the torment which follows."

Since Solomon was the king, he could arrange pleasure for himself. He could have all kinds of entertainment provided by jesters, singers, actors, and other performers. He eventually accumulated one thousand wives and became the only man in history who could honestly say to any one of his thousand wives, "Honey, you're one in a thousand." Finally, he came to a conclusion about pleasure: "Whatever my eyes desired I did not keep from them; I kept my heart from no pleasure, for my heart found pleasure in all my toil, and this was my reward for all my toil. Then I considered all that my hands had done and the toil I had spent in doing it, and behold, all was vanity and a striving after wind, and there was nothing to be gained under the sun" (Eccl. 2:10-11).

So he began to wonder what else might possibly bring him happiness and decided that wealth might be the answer. This is typical of many modern men. They feel that the best thing they can give their families is money. They put forth their greatest energy in making more and more money. Money becomes a substitute for the gift of themselves. This philosophy is typified by the farmer who said that he really didn't want much out of life. All he ever cared about owning was "just all of the land that ever touches my land!"

Solomon became so wealthy that stories began to spread about his riches. The queen of Sheba came to visit Solomon's court in order to satisfy her own curiosity concerning the stories she had heard about his wealth. She left saying, "The half was not told me."

But Solomon found out about the uncertainty of riches. Much

is recorded about this matter in chapters 3 through 6. First, there is the lack of assurance of having a wise successor to inherit one's fortune. Second, one's life is wholly in the power of an arbitrary God. Moreover, injustice in the law courts takes money. Fourth, taxation takes a large share of riches. Success causes jealousy and loss of friends. Sixth, the acquisition of wealth does not bring satisfaction. The more one makes, the more one spends. Last, a rich man is sometimes denied by God the power to live and enjoy his possessions. Some of these observations seem up to date. Yet they are all there in this old, old book. Solomon concluded in chapter 5 and verse 10, "He who loves money will not be satisfied with money; nor he who loves wealth, with gain: this also is vanity."

Solomon sought elsewhere for happiness and decided that perhaps if he could just become famous, widely known, loved and respected by his people, fame would bring happiness. Many young people have a similar priority. During those years of junior high, high school, and even college, the greatest thing in all the world is popularity. Yet some people who are elected as most popular in the class make little use of their lives and become very unpopular with themselves in the years that ensue. Solomon gave his conclusion on fame in chapter 11, "Rejoice, O young man, in your youth, and let your heart cheer you in the days of your youth; walk in the ways of your heart and the sight of your eyes. But know that for all these things God will bring you into judgment" (v. 9).

By this time Solomon was beginning to get older and his health was failing. He began to think that, if he could only regain his health, he would be happy. Many of us have the idea that longevity brings the greatest happiness in life. Yet someone has said, "It is not the days in your life that matter, it's the life in your days that really counts." The poets Shelley and Keats lived only about thirty years and yet made their contribution to enrich all our lives. Even our Lord Jesus Christ lived only about thirty-three years and who could say he didn't live long enough to accomplish his mission. Even health doesn't guarantee happiness. Some people try to get happy ("high") on drugs. Others find they can achieve happiness through conversation, laughter, and even religion. Solomon's long conclusion about health is most understandable from *The Living Bible*.

For there will come a time when your limbs will tremble with age, and your strong legs will become weak, and your teeth will be too few to do their work, and there will be blindness, too. Then let your lips be tightly closed while eating, when your teeth are gone! And you will waken at dawn with the first note of the birds; but you yourself will be deaf and tuneless, with quavering voice. You will be afraid of heights and of falling—a white-haired, withered old man, dragging himself along: without sexual desire, standing at death's door, and nearing his everlasting home as the mourners go along the streets (Eccl. 12:3-5).

No, Solomon concluded that happiness was achieved by something else. In the twelfth and last chapter of his book, he said there are many things that he did not understand in this life, but one thing stood out clearly: when his faith in God was strong, he was happier than when it was weak. The existential frustrations of life make one grateful for eternal life (12:7). Even if this life on earth is all that there is, it pays to serve God. One is better off following God's principles because devotion to God makes one happier. In 12:13 Solomon says, "The end of the matter; all has been heard," and he gives two suggestions: "Fear God, and keep his commandments; for this is whole duty of man."

During your illness, when you have time on your hands, questions that you have been able to put off during the busy days of your healthy life now march in one after another and claim some of your attention. I hope you will remember the words of Solomon as found in the Book of Ecclesiastes and that somehow these words will be of help to you as you face some perhaps unanswerable yet inevitable questions about happiness in your life.

The Touch of Faith

One day Jesus was on a busy errand to minister to the sick son of a nobleman when he suddenly stopped and asked the crowd, "Who was it that touched me?" This is an electrifying question—Christ stopping in response to the touch of a poor, nameless woman. It is a provocative question when you think about it. These words march right into the vestibule of your heart and knock on the door and say, "Who touched me? Did you?"

The incident took place in one of the crowded, crooked city streets in Jerusalem. At the request of Jairus, a ruler of the synagogue, Jesus was on his way to restore a little girl's health, the daughter of Jairus. But Christ, even on a busy errand, was not too busy to help her.

The woman who touched Jesus was a woman whose name we do not know. Some have thought that her name was Veronica; others have thought her name was Martha. We simply do not know what her name was. She remains anonymous. We can assume that for some people she functioned in the role of daughter, and perhaps sister, wife, mother, or aunt. We only know that she was a woman in pain.

We don't know where she came from either. Eusebius, the ancient historian, records a tradition that she was a Gentile from Ceasarea Philippi. This seems reasonable enough since a Jewess would scarcely have ventured into a crowd believing that she would contaminate everyone that she touched with her ceremonial pollution. Nevertheless, we cannot be sure where she called home.

We don't know anything about her history other than this particular incident. There are some stories or legends that may or may not be true. They are interesting though. One of these was that she maintained the innocency of Christ before Pilate. Another story has it that she wiped his face with a napkin as he was on the road to Calvary bearing his cross. A third legend says that she erected a memorial for Jesus in Caesarea Philippi, her hometown.

Albeit the fact of the matter is that she simply is an anonymous woman in the Scripture. We don't know her name, her home, or anything about her. We can learn a very important lesson from her: that we are never lost from God—even in a crowd, even in the midst of those who are thronging about his Son. Our identity, our problems, and our needs are never unknown to God. I think we can also learn that like this anonymous woman, we, too, can come to Christ in our need without fame or wealth or education or anything in particular except our needs.

This was a woman who was very troubled. She had a chronic hemorrhage for twelve years that was unmentionable in public. This made her very timid about openly discussing her disease. Today she would have been diagnosed as having a condition of menorrhagia (excessive blood loss during menstruation) or dysmenorrhea (painful menstruation). She was ceremonially unclean according to the Levitical law of the Old Testament (Lev. 15:25-30) and was legally forbidden to touch another person or to let another person touch her. You might consider, for instance, how a Pharisee might have reacted if he had known her condition when she had touched him, making him ceremonially unfit to enter the Temple and worship.

She had consulted many doctors and undergone many treatments. She had suffered much as a result of it. The Scriptures say this. Let me give you a few examples of some of the typical cures for her disease in New Testament times. One recorded in the Talmud and resorted to in extreme cases was to "set her in the place where two ways meet (a crossroad) and let her hold a cup of wine in her right hand and then let someone come up from behind and frighten her by saying, 'Arise from thy flux!'" This was supposed to scare the disease away. In those days physicians were apt to prescribe doses of curious concoctions made from ashes of burnt wolf skulls, stag's horns, the heads of mice, the eyes of crab, owls' brains, and the livers of frogs. This was to be taken orally to bring about a cure in their patients. For dysentery, powered horses teeth were administered orally. A head cold was supposed to be cured by kissing a mule's nose. These were typical treatments that were used in New Testament times. So, I think we ought to be able to believe the Scriptures when it says that she "had suffered much under many physicians, and had spent all that she had, and was no better but rather grew worse" (Mark 5:26). One of the poets tried to sum up her sentiments with these words:

> I have tried and tried in vain,
> Many ways to ease my pain;
> Now all other hope is past,
> Only this is left at last:
> Here before thy cross I lie;
> Here I live or here I die.

—AUTHOR UNKNOWN

This lady decided to bring her troubles to "The Great Physician." We should, too. She must have heard stories about Jesus of Nazareth and his healing the sick. Even though she had gone to many physicians, she took hope and decided to consult one more. The lady had faith, but her faith was a trustful expectancy tinged with supposition. She may not have thought of Jesus as divine and probably never dreamed who he really was. She believed few, if any, of the intellectual tenets now incorporated into the creeds and statements of faith of today's churches. Faith is often tested by the difficulties it overcomes. She set out on a long trek to find this so-called "Great Physician." She asked different people in Palestine who directed her eventually to the place where Jesus was. She found him in the midst of a crowd on the way to make a house call in response to an urgent request from Jairus, whose daughter was ill. She

wondered how she could get his attention, tell him the nature of
her disease, and ask him to help her. As she pondered she
decided not to take a direct approach at all. She had probably
heard the story about Christ's touching a leper and curing him
by his touch (Matt. 8:3). She must have decided that if Christ
could heal a leper by touching him, perhaps she could find healing by secretly and quietly touching Christ. She was actually rather
ingenious in thinking up this new idea. (There is always room for
new ideas, new ways, and new methods in God's work.) She
moved forward in the crowd toward Christ. As she came closer
she might have thought, "Ok, I'm going to touch him, but where
should I touch him? I'm close enough now that I could tiptoe
and reach over the heads of these others and touch his head.
Maybe I shouldn't touch his head because that would seem
rather irreverent. If I can get closer I could reach between the
people and touch his hand, but that would be too familiar."

The Scriptures seem to be very plain about what she did
touch. In older translations of the Bible it says that she touched
the "hem" of his garment. But the newer versions translate the
Greek word as *fringe*. The Jews wore tassels or fringes of
hyacinth blue attached to the four corners of their upper
garment. These were called the "Jewish tallith or zizth." One
hung over each shoulder, one was in the center of the chest, and
one between the shoulders in the back. This was a symbol of
their faith. She probably touched one of Jesus' tassels. She
touched it and suddenly felt something.

Jesus also felt something. And we turn our thoughts from the
unknown woman to the known man in the story. When Jesus felt
her touch, he started asking over and over again, "Who touched
me?" Finally the crowd stopped and grew quiet, which took a
while. Jesus continued to ask, "Who touched me?" His disciples
argued with him about the appropriateness of his question. Jesus
persisted in giving a public invitation for the one who had
secretly had faith, touched him, and been cured to come forward

publicly and acknowledge what had happened so as to give God the glory.

The woman found the Great Physician to be quite competent. He healed her while many physicians had failed. Yet he didn't want her to go away having received a ministry to her physical condition only. Jesus treated the whole person and wanted to deal with her spiritual needs as well as her physical needs. This is a current theme in medicine again today. Physicians treat chaplains as colleagues and members of the healing team, recognizing that spiritual needs are important.

Jesus asked her to come forward, and she did. She tried to trust secretly but was called on for a public confession. Jesus said to her, "Daughter, your faith has made you well; go in peace, and be healed of your disease" (Mark 5:34). This is the only biblical recording that we have of Jesus using the endearing word *daughter* to any woman. He said to her that she was ever after to continue in peace. We work from our moment of faith. We go peacefully working, hoping that others, too, will find faith through our life and our witness.

Well, these are the facts of the record. The story, of course, is now history. The woman represents a sinner who has been drained to hopelessness by sin and then in despair reaches out for Christ. Are you in touch with Christ? We, figuratively speaking, are in the crowd surrounding him but are you in touch with Christ? The woman thought that getting in touch with Christ was worth a try. She was no stranger to failure, so she put forth an effort. She touched him, and so can we. The human touch does have the power to arrest God's attention. Of course, you are justified in looking for direction on the lid or some instruction for taking this spiritual medicine. The Scriptures are quite plain about them. Repent, confess, believe, receive. These are the words we use which means that we somehow, some way, get in touch with Christ or allow him to get in touch with us through an act of faith and personally inviting him into our lives and into our midst.

Spiritual Wisdom

No one is born wise; one can only become wise. Yet neither is age a guarantee of wisdom. It has often been said, "There is no fool like an old fool." Some people have the idea that all the knowledge of the Bible is known. Others say confidently that all knowledge is to be found in the Bible. It is tragic when people feel that they now know all they will ever need to know. Yet some drop out of church as though they had learned all that the church has to offer.

When we get sick, I think we do some reconsideration of the whole question of knowledge. How much do I know and do I know enough already to get me through the circumstances of being ill? Or should I perhaps try to learn something more about what it is to be sick and to get well or to linger? I think that being ill reopens the whole question of spiritual wisdom. We may suddenly find ourselves assuming again the role of a student and trying to learn something significant about this new experience in our lives. No two sicknesses are alike.

There are, of course, different types of students. The Jewish Mishnah speaks of four types of students: the sponge who just absorbs everything, the funnel who lets knowledge in at one end and out at the other, the strainer who lets out the wine of knowledge and retains the dregs, and the sieve who lets out the coarse and keeps the fine flour.

If you feel that during your illness you have become a student again and have felt something of this inner need and urge to learn something more about how to understand your illness, then I would like to point you to a comforting verse of Scripture: "If any of you lacks wisdom, let him ask God, who gives to all men generously and without reproaching, and it will be given him" (Jas. 1:5). This Scripture indicates that there are three ways to seek after this kind of extra wisdom that we need to get us through an illness.

First of all, recognize that you lack wisdom. Too many of us trust in our own human knowledge and intellect for wisdom. You may have seen the cartoon of the young person in a college graduation robe being given his college diploma that has "AB" written on it. The world is depicted in the background saying, "Now come with me, and I'll teach you the rest of your *ABC's.*" A college sophomore may think that he or she knows everything but a college senior is not so sure.

It has often been repeated that "a little knowledge is a dangerous thing!" Thomas Huxley has written, "If a little knowledge is dangerous, where is the man who has so much as to be out of danger?" Certainly, when a new experience in life is thrust upon us, we feel our need for more wisdom to understand it better.

Those in the professions recognize their lack of wisdom. For instance, today's engineer is said to spend 40 percent of his time keeping up with new developments in his field. And consider the current advances in the medical field. Ninety percent of the medicines most used today were completely unknown just ten years ago.

You and I must also work hard to keep up with our bodies and our experiences if we are to understand them. Jesus said to his disciples one time, "I have many things to say to you, but you cannot bear them now" (John 16:12). Hopefully you are ready to find the meaning in your illness. But first, you must be like Socrates who said, "The Delphic oracle said that I was the wisest of all the Greeks. It is because that I alone, of all the Greeks, know that I know nothing."

The second idea in this verse of Scripture is that, having recognized our lack of wisdom, we should ask God for wisdom. Now, it is easy to misunderstand this verse at precisely this point. Some students have experimented with this verse by praying for wisdom rather than studying for it. We all know that this doesn't work. Some of these students are a little bit like blotters. They soak everything up but they get it all backwards.

Even some ministers boast or at least imply that God gives

them every word that they say in a sermon. There is a story about a German minister named Heinrich. One day two of his colleagues both told glowing stories about how they had done no preparation for their sermons the previous Sunday but simply depended on God, and each had delivered a great sermon. Heinrich, who was listening to them, thought perhaps he should at least try that method, for it seemed to indicate that his friends were more dedicated and dependent upon God than he. So the next Sunday morning he prayed very hard as his congregation sang and then waited for his sermon to come to him for he had made no preparation. Later he told his two ministerial friends about it. He said, "When I didn't prepare for my sermon, the only words that God would give to me when I would pray were, 'Heinrich, you're lazy!'"

We do need to realize that we lack wisdom and then, like Solomon, ask God for wisdom. Solomon in his dream (2 Chron. 1:9-12) could have asked God for anything. He could have asked for wealth, honor, revenge on his enemies, or for long life. Instead, he simply asked for wisdom that he might rule his people well. He did not presume himself to be wise but asked for the ability to distinguish good from evil. God blessed his request and gave him wisdom.

The word *Christian* is one of our English words that is in the diminutive form. The "ian" on the end of the word *Christ* makes it mean literally small or little Christ. Perhaps you and I should also try to be Solomonians or little Solomons who have realized our lack of wisdom and have asked God to help us become wise.

What is this spiritual wisdom that I am suggesting we ask God for? It is not a conglomeration of factual knowledge. It is not simply formal education which can be little more than the passing of knowledge from the notebook of the professor to the notebook of the student, without going through the head of either. It is a kind of common sense. According to Samuel Taylor Coleridge, "Common sense in the uncommon degree is what the world calls wisdom." Knowledge may be gained by study, but wisdom seems to come from life's experiences as God helps us to understand them and profit from them. Wisdom is assimilating and applying knowledge through personality. There are two ways of learning: study and experience. Study is formal, purposive, and productive. Experience is often accidental and informal, but it keeps pounding in on us day by day until we get the message.

Spiritual wisdom is what faith was to Paul: being in union with God and estimating the values of life from God's standpoint. Spiritual wisdom is what hope was to Peter: a vision of the future as God intends it. It is what love was to John: the consummation of fellowship with God and the brethren. It is the essence of Christian life: the art of living life to its fullest. Spiritual wisdom is a gift of God that is given through prayer and meditation.

The third point made in our Scripture passage is that we should believe that we will receive wisdom when we ask for it. Jesus said, "Therefore I tell you, whatever you ask in prayer, believe that you receive it, and you will" (Mark 11:24). God can give us new knowledge as we keep our minds open, as we think for ourselves, and as we look for new knowledge in order to assimilate our experiences in life into a meaningful whole. Old dogs can be taught new tricks. Pavlov, the Russian psychologist, proved this in the early 1900s.

During the Renaissance, people began to think for themselves in matters of science and literature. During the Reformation, people began to think for themselves in matters of religion.

In the incident recorded in Acts 4, Peter and John were so full of divine wisdom that even though they were obviously "ignorant and unlearned men," the Sanhedrin recognized that they had been with Jesus.

We need the wisdom of the Alcoholics Anonymous prayer.

> Oh God: give me the courage to change the things I
>   can change,
> The ability to accept the things I cannot change,
> And the wisdom to know the difference.

Spiritual wisdom begins with reverence for God, the beginning of all wisdom. Spiritual wisdom is not just cleverness or cunning. It is the abundant life promised by Jesus.

Divine wisdom will come from grappling with our own moral, intellectual, and emotional problems. It will come from relating the Christian faith to our own lives pointedly and forcefully. It will come from being our own physicians before we seek to cure others. This involves a process of honest self-examination so that we ask less, "Will it work?" and more often, "Is it true, or is it right?" Divine wisdom demands great humility, to the point of saying, "I don't know" or even "I am wrong," hard words for anyone to pronounce.

Illness is an enigma. It is hard to know why we become sick and why we don't get better. Yet, there is something to be learned from illness. Alexandre Dumas said, "All human wisdom is summed up in two words: wait and hope." There is meaning in illness for the person who has the courage to ask God about it, or to talk to the chaplain or others about it.

The writer of Proverbs assures us,
Yes, if you cry out for insight
    and raise your voice for understanding,
if you seek it like silver
    and search for it as for hidden treasures;
then you will understand the fear of the Lord
    and find the knowledge of God.
For the Lord gives wisdom;
    from his mouth comes knowledge and understanding (Prov. 2:3-6).

Settled in the Sanctuary

I would like to tell you a story which may be helpful and encouraging to you in your time of illness.

When I first became acquainted with this hospitalized patient, he began to talk about religion, reciting to me some of the traditions of his belief and assuring me that he believed in God. The man said that he had tried to live a Christian life and was the kind of person who had taken his religion very seriously. He had tried to be Christian at home, at work, in his neighborhood, and wherever he found himself.

As I continued to listen, he began to tell me of a time in his life when he had almost lost his personal faith. He explained that the cause of his dangerous brush with apostasy was the apparent prosperity of the wicked. It occurred to him that he had more than his share of trouble and nonchurchgoers seemed to have fewer problems than he did.

He had tried to be a good example to one of his neighbors who obviously was not a believer and never went to church. It seemed that nothing bad ever happened to this guy. He had a good job and got one promotion after another. He liked to talk about his savings account and show everyone his bank balance which was always quite large. He also liked to brag about his good health. His neighbor's boastfulness really irked the hospitalized patient.

The patient told me, "Here I was trying to make a good impression on my neighbors, but they all seemed to follow this other fellow. He's the real leader in the neighborhood. He's outgoing, and he is not afraid to take a risk and try to do something. He had a big weiner roast at his house and invited all the neighbors. Nearly everybody came. A lot of people did more drinking than I thought they should have. My neighbor even encouraged people to get drunk by saying, "How can God know?" But everyone seemed to have a good time. I just never have had the courage to invite all the neighbors to my home and try to be an example of godly living."

As the patient's irritation increased, he had to admit that he wasn't going to church as regularly as he had before. Just any little thing could come up, and he would use this as an excuse for not going to church.

Not long before his hospitalization, he did go to church one Sunday morning. His doubts about his religion were weighing very heavily on his mind at the time. In Sunday School he talked with more candor about his problem than he meant to, and to his surprise a lady told him afterwards that what he had said helped her with a similar problem.

Then he went into the sanctuary for the worship service. His pastor gave a sermon on Isaiah 6. The king had died when Isaiah was a young man, and Isaiah was really burdened down with grief, just as our entire nation was upset by the death of President Kennedy in our country. Young Isaiah, in the despair of bereavement, wandered into the Temple where he began to pray and express to God how badly he felt. Then Isaiah had a religious experience that changed his outlook and his opinion of himself. The pastor giving the sermon made it clear that prosperity may only last for a day or two, but building a good reputation and having a good character is something that is worthwhile in this life and in the next. As Victor Hugo said, "Success is a very hideous thing, and its resemblance to merit deceives man."

A wonderful thing happened to this patient in that worship service at church because, as he listened to his pastor preach, he began to understand some things. He realized that his neighbor and others who don't serve God and yet have prosperity could lose all their possessions or even their own lives in a minute. It came to him that even though these people may think that everything is wonderful, they are actually on slippery ground and could fall quickly. But the patient had his faith to stabilize his life and help him find meaning in his life situation.

Then the patient told me about a dream that his neighbor had told him about. The neighbor dreamed that his own house had completely burned to the ground and that the patient's house was still standing. He said he hadn't thought much about the dream until he heard the sermon and was trying to put all of this together. He decided that maybe the dream meant that his neighbor didn't feel quite as secure as he acted.

The patient trusted in God and was aware that God gave leadership to his life. God gave a dimension of guidance and counsel to him in everyday decisions and in the big decisions he had made like his vocational choice and his marital choice. He also felt sure that God had a reward for him that finally would come after this life was over.

The patient wrote a poem about his thoughts. I would like to quote part of it.

> Whom have I in heaven but thee?
>> And there is nothing upon earth that I desire besides thee.
> My flesh and my heart may fail,
>> but God is the strength of my heart and my portion forever.

> For lo, those who are far from thee shall perish;
>> Thou dost put an end to those who are false to thee.
> But for me it is good to be near God;
>> I have made the Lord God my refuge,
>> that I may tell of all thy works.

Now I have a personal confession to make. I haven't been writing about a patient at all. I have been telling you the story about the writer of the seventy-third Psalm (vv. 25-28). I have talked about the psalmist as though he were a hospital patient. The psalm does indicate that he had been sick. In a very human and confessional way the psalmist tells us about his problem with his faith. But then he went into the sanctuary of God and had the kind of experience that I have described, much like that of Isaiah. His problems were settled in the sanctuary.

Dr. Kyle Yates, an Old Testament scholar, called this seventy-third Psalm the greatest of them all. I think it can and should speak to our hearts in a very modern way these days. I suggest that you read it thoughtfully.

The Personal Touch

"He stretched out his hand, and touched him" (Luke 5:13).

Jesus touched a leper. And in this case, it seemed that nothing less than Jesus' personal touch would do. Yet, when Jesus stretched forth his hand and touched the leper that day at the leper's request, he was bridging a great chasm that had long before been fixed in Hebrew history.

Six feet away was as close as any leper could ever approach another healthy human being. Lepers were considered to be untouchable. If a leper suspected that someone (not knowing that he was a leper) was about to come nearer to him than six feet away, then the leper was required by law to yell out a warning, saying, "Unclean, I'm unclean!" If a leper so much as stuck his head inside a doorway to see if anyone were at home, then everyone present in the house was considered to be unclean and contaminated. In fact, of the sixty-one contacts listed in the Old Testament law that defiled a person, touching a leper is second in the list. Only touching the dead was considered to be more contaminating. Yet the Scriptures tell us that Jesus reached out his hand and touched the leper (Mark 1:41).

It seems to me that God has done for all of us something similar to what Jesus did for the sick leper. For God, in a sense, has stretched out his "hand" toward the world by sending Christ his Son and has personally touched our world. God bridged the great chasm between the divine and the human when he sent his Son Jesus to have personal contact with us. The personal touch of God-in-Christ conveyed some things that the world needs to acknowledge.

When Jesus stretched out his hand and touched the leper that day, he was indicating to the leper, "Your life is worth living." The leper undoubtedly had a lot of questions in his mind about that. He had the kind of disease that cut him off from contact with people. His disease caused him to live the life of a hermit outside the city walls. He was unable to work and support his family or even himself. The leper must have wondered often if his life was worth living. Then Jesus touched him affirmatively.

By coming to this world, Jesus was telling all of us that all our lives are worth living. Jesus came to this world as a baby and grew normally to adulthood. His infancy included being held and cuddled tenderly in his mother's arms. He also experienced childhood and studied at the Hebrew synagogue school. He knew what it was to have a skinned knee and to try to learn his lessons. We have in the Bible a brief glimpse of Jesus at twelve during his pilgrimage to Jerusalem with his parents. Jesus knew what it was to be a young person and to be faced with the typical problems seeking an identity and choosing a vocation and life-style. He knew what it was to learn a trade and to support a family through labor because this fell his lot as the oldest son when Joseph died. He experienced the stress of trying to help his mother look after the family, make decisions, and earn a living. Through Christ, God touched man and placed his benediction on everyday life. For Jesus touched all of life.

Jesus was a man, even though at the same time, he also was God. That's very difficult for us to understand. Donald Bailey, the late Scottish theologian, asked us in one of his books to imagine a street scene in which Jesus was talking to a crowd of people. Someone caught one of Jesus' disciples by the arm and asked, "Who is that man?" Bailey points out that not even the most astute of Jesus' disciples would have replied, "Oh, that's not a man at all. That's God." Yet in Christ, God visited mankind, touched our normal human existence, and helped us to find meaning within it.

The second thing I think we can notice in Jesus' touch of the leper is that people are worth saving. The leper must have wondered about that because there were many people who must have thought his life was worthless. Few people would have given him any hope for recovery. Still, Jesus seemed to think that this man's life was worth saving.

This seems to be the reason God visited humanity in Christ. Christ didn't come to the earth to perform a bit of divine razzmatazz or to perform fantastic feats of divine magic to prove that God was still the master of the miraculous arts. Jesus was not sent to entertain us. God sent Jesus to the world because he was so sure that all persons are worth saving. Christ touched life personally in order to say that all persons are worthy in the sight of God.

Karl Barth has been called the most prominent of Protestant theologians in the twentieth century. Karl Barth lived in Zurich, Switzerland, and taught there at the university. He wrote one huge volume of theology after another. As Barth's theological expertise was more and more widely recognized, he began to receive many invitations to come to different cities to make speeches. He was even invited to come to our country and speak to huge crowds. But each invitation was answered in just about the same way. Karl Barth would write back, "I am sorry. As much as I would like to accept your kind invitation, I have a previous engagement."

People began to wonder what Karl Barth's previous engagements were. Students who traveled to Switzerland to learn from him found out. Karl Barth had committed himself to preach on Sundays to the prisoners in the local jail. He did this regularly and with great interest and concern. A number of these sermons were later published in a book entitled *Deliverance to the Captives*. Each sermon began with these words, "My dear brothers and sisters in Christ."

Karl Barth considered that particular aspect of humanity that most of us might think is the lowest class—the prisoners—to be his brothers and sisters in Christ. And in the same way that Karl Barth considered the lowliest person worth visiting, God believed that all people were worth visiting and worth saving.

The other idea that I think we can get out of this Scripture passage is that Christ is worth knowing. Certainly this leper must have felt that of all the people he had ever known in all of his life, Jesus Christ was most worth knowing. Jesus Christ had the word of life. Once when multitudes were following him, he gave a sermon that contained what many of his followers called "hard sayings." From that time on, many people turned aside and stopped following him. Jesus asked his own disciples, "Will ye also go away?" Peter spoke for the group by saying, "Lord, to whom shall we go? You have the words of eternal life."

Jesus Christ was a kind of word from God to people about life.

In Christ, God seemed to be saying, "This is what life's about. If you want to know how I intend life to be lived, then look at Christ's life, and you'll have a good example." Jesus' life showed that God loves all people in all situations in life. The leper certainly felt that Christ was worth knowing and those of us who have felt the personal touch of God in our lives feel that Christ is worth knowing. It is one thing for us to know about God, to hear about God, and to read books about God, but it's something altogether different to feel that we somehow have come to know God and have felt his personal touch in our lives. That's the thing that makes life worth living and makes our lives worth saving and makes Christ worth knowing.

Somehow we can get in touch with the Almighty God who stands ready to touch our lives through Christ even as Christ stood ready to touch the leper's life that day. When we invite God into our lives through prayer, he is able to "touch" us personally. It is the personal touch of God in our lives that makes our lives worth living and helps to reassure us in our hearts that Christ is worth knowing.

With Christ in Life's Storms

On that day, when evening had come, he said to them, "Let us go across to the other side." And leaving the crowd, they took him with them in the boat, just as he was. And other boats were with him. And a great storm of wind arose, and the waves beat into the boat, so that the boat was already filling. But he was in the stern, asleep on the cushion; and they woke him and said to him, "Teacher, do you not care if we perish?" And he awoke and rebuked the wind, and said to the sea, "Peace! Be still!" And the wind ceased, and there was a great calm. He said to them, "Why are you so afraid? Have you no faith?" And they were filled with awe, and said to one another, "Who then is this, that even wind and sea obey him?" (Mark 4:35-41).

There are several lessons we can learn from this passage of
Scripture. There are several things that you and I can apply to
our own lives about this sudden storm that came in the life of
Jesus and the disciples. None of us ever really expect a storm to
come. None of us ever really prepare much for a storm. We
never really plan for it and prepare for it. We never plan or
prepare for the storm of sickness either. We never invite it into
our life. It simply comes, unannounced and unexpectedly and
makes its presence felt.

Jesus and his disciples were not expecting the storm, and yet
it came. The wonderful part about it was, from the point of view
of the disciples, that Christ was already with them in the boat
when the storm came. They had met him during the earlier,
calmer seasons of their lives. They had already invited him into
their lives. They had already left all and followed him." They
followed him wherever he went. They studied his life. They had
become his disciples. They walked in the way of the Lord. They
followed in his footsteps. They helped in his ministry. As a
matter of fact, they had continued with him even when many
others had turned aside, no longer to follow him. These men
continued to walk with the Lord even though many storms had
already come: sudden storms and severe enough that many of his
followers had been turned aside. They had said concerning
certain of his teachings, "These are hard sayings. Who could
hear them? Who can do them?" And they stopped following. But
these disciples continued to follow Jesus. It reminds me of the
words of the German poet, Goethe who said, "Tell me with
whom thou art found, and I shall tell thee who thou art." It is
true that something can be known about us by the company we
keep. These men were following Jesus' request to take him
across the lake in the boat that he might continue his work on the
other side.

Such storms do come to each of us, if not literally then
figuratively. Since all of us are going to have our bouts with
sickness through life and finally with death, then like the

disciples, we need to be sure that we have Christ with us in the boat even before the storms come. Any sailor or most fishermen could tell you that during a storm is the worst of all times to try to take someone else into the boat. That is dangerous, even if the person that you are taking into the boat is a pilot to guide you to safety.

Jesus was with them in the boat, but nevertheless the storm came. It's a mistake for us to assume that if we are Christians we will be excused from the storms of life. And yet this is a mistake that is very widely made. Many people who become ill assume that God is sending their sickness upon them as punishment for something bad that they've done. I really think this idea is poor theology. Nevertheless, I am constantly amazed at how widespread such an idea has become. God loves us at all times. God accepts us at all times. It is true that because he does give us such freedom as human beings that we sometimes get ourselves into difficulties. We drive too fast or we climb too high or we are not careful or cautious enough about our eating habits and sleeping habits, and so forth. Sometimes we work too hard or expose ourselves for too long to severities of the weather. Yet, I have trouble finding evidence in the Bible that God himself sends physical afflictions upon us in direct punishment for our sins. The storm came upon the disciples in no way for that kind of reason. The Lord Jesus himself was with them in the boat, and yet the storm came. Just like many storms come upon us even though we have Christ with us in our lives. This is no reflection on our Christianity. We shouldn't consider it to be such. Rather, we should just thank God Almighty that we have Christ with us and that we are with him in our journey of life.

During the time of the storm, we can pray. We can call on God for help. We can sense his presence with us, because we may as well face it; the storms of life will come to us. Sickness may come. Disability may come. Sorrow and bereavement will come. This is our lot in life at one time or another. Disappointments and frustrations will come. All of the things we hope for, plan for, certainly will not come through. We will experience anxiety and loss. The storms will come, but with Christ in the boat with us we can be much more confident during the storm.

The storm that came as recorded in the Scriptures did not in any way disprove Christ's deity. It, rather, served to emphasize it. Though storms that come in our lives are no kind of proof of our waywardness or of the long distance between us and God, perhaps, like in our biblical story, the storms that come in our life can simply help us to demonstrate to our neighbors what it means to be a Christian.

When the storm came, the disciples did what you and I usually do, they prayed. They prayed during the storm. And you and I also pray when the storms come. We call out to God to help us. We call out to God because we believe he hears us. We call out to God because we believe he can and will help us.

The prayers that the disciples prayed were imperfect prayers. They weren't perfect at all. They uttered a purely selfish cry, "We perish." In fact as Mark puts it, they asked Jesus, "Teacher, do you not care if we perish?" That is a selfish prayer, and yet a very typical prayer of a person in distress. There was no concern in their prayer for Jesus' safety. There was no concern for the future work of God's kingdom. Yet, they did pray. They did call out to God. They called out to Christ and through him to God. So we could agree upon one thing, they were in dead earnest. Christ doesn't condition hearing and answering our prayers on our perfection. He conditions his hearing and his response upon our earnestness. If we pray sincerely, then we can have the confidence that our prayer will be heard.

As a matter of fact, the disciples seemed to get a perfect answer to their rather imperfect prayers. Jesus dealt with their difficulties. They were greatly disturbed over the raging sea and the howling winds. So Jesus tried to give them what they wanted. He spoke and said, "Peace! Be still!" We have always interpreted this to mean that he was speaking directly to the winds and to the waves and commanding them to be quiet.

Perhaps we have missed the main thrust of what the Lord had to say. Jesus was, as usual, far more concerned about the fear in the hearts of the disciples than he was about the physical elements. Perhaps he was directing his words most of all to them, "Peace, be still." Jesus was calm and at peace even in the midst of a raging storm.

As we have the story, the storm did cease. The disciples were given what they wanted: a quiet sea. They wanted a peaceful voyage across the lake. The storm had emphasized their lack of faith. Jesus dealt with their doubts. They had the Lord with them in the boat, but still they feared for their lives and cried out to him. He rebuked them in order to give them faith. Where is your faith? Why are you so afraid? But they ended this whole episode with a new conception of who he was. Mark summarized it for us when he said, "They feared exceedingly, and said one to another, What manner of man is this, that even the wind and the sea obey him?" (4:41, KJV). I expect they had a long discussion about Jesus and who he was in the calmness that followed the storm.

There really is no calmness ever to be compared with the kind of calmness that follows a furious storm. Yet, even when life's sea is calm, we need Christ as our pilot lest we drift off our course. We need him with us when the storms come lest we make a shipwreck of our lives.

You and I need to realize that in the midst of the storm Christ is with us. If we pray—no matter how we word our prayers—if they are genuine and sincere, the Lord hears them. And the Lord speaks to our needs. He is most of all interested in us, his people, the highest type of his creation. Sometimes, in order to help us he may even deal with things around us as he did in the case of the disciples. But the Lord is with us even during the storm. Trust God in Christ. The sea of life is his. He made it. After the storm you will know him better and find peace. Remember the prayer of the British fisherman: "Keep me, O God; my boat is so small, and thy ocean is so great."

Part V

Prayers
of Faith

The God of All Ages

O God of my infancy,
The Age of Grace;
I thank you for the
Undemanding love
Which came to me
From my parents.

O God of my toddling years,
The Age of Works;
I thank you for the
Kind, firm teachings
On timeliness, orderliness, and cleanliness
Which came to me
From my parents.

O God of my venturing years,
The Age of Family Romance;
I thank you for the
Love generated in me
For my parent of the opposite sex,
And for the understanding
Of my parent of the same sex.

O God of my grade school years,
The Age of Friendships;
I thank you for the

Teachers and peers
Who broadened my perspectives
And taught me how to compete.

O God of my puberty,
The Age of Discovery;
I thank you for the
Newfound importance of
A close friend,
And for the fearful
Changes in my body
Which signaled my identity.

O God of my adolescence,
The Age of Struggle;
I thank you for the
Opposite sex
And your help in my
Contention with my
Identity and independence.

O God of my young adulthood,
The Age of Adjustment;
I thank you for my
Physical and intellectual powers
And for your guidance
In my selection of
A vocation and a spouse.

O God of my middle adulthood,
The Age of Achievement;
I thank you for my
Family of both origin and progeny,
For the success I attained,
And for your assistance
Through the mid-life crisis.

O God of my later adulthood,
The Age of Conservation;
I thank you for my
Health and my memories,
And for your presence with me
In all of life
And in death.

—RICHARD DAYRINGER

A Nurse's Prayer

I dedicate myself to thee,
O Lord, my God, this work
  I undertake
Alone in thy great name,
  and for thy sake.
In ministering to suffering
  I would learn
The sympathy that in thy
  heart did burn.

Take, then, mine eyes, and
  teach them to perceive
The ablest way each sick
  one to relieve
Guide thou my hands, that
  e'en their touch may prove
The gentleness and aptness
  born of love.

Bless thou my feet, and
  while they softly tread
May faces smile on many a
  sufferer's bed.

Touch thou my lips, guide
  thou my tongue,
Give me a work in sermon
  for each one.

Clothe me with patience,
  strength all tasks to bear,
Crown me with hope and love,
  which know no fear,
And faith, that coming face
  to face with death
Shall e'en inspire with joy
  the dying breath.

All through the arduous day
  my actions guide,
All through the lonely
  night watch by my side,
So I shall wake refreshed,
  with strength to pray,
Work in me, through me,
  with me, Lord, this day.

—AUTHOR UNKNOWN

A Christmas Prayer

Dear God,

It's near the end of the year and we, like Mary and Joseph in their time, are trying to get to Bethlehem. We surmise that their journey was long, bumpy, and trying. We know that ours is. In fact, there are moments when we get so weary that we seriously doubt that we will be able to make it to Bethlehem this year.

For a long time the hospital for the insane in London, Saint Mary's of Bethlehem, has been called Bedlam for short. Help us not to wind up in Bedlam this year. We really want to make it to Bethlehem as did Mary and Joseph.

In your great wisdom, O God, and at a time when the world was in great desperation, you slipped in with a Child. Help us to find Bethlehem and discover the Baby who grew to become the Savior during the Christmas season this year.

In the name of the Christ of Christmas, we pray. Amen.

—RICHARD DAYRINGER

A Prayer for Inner Peace

O Lord, this hospital is a strange place. The day is filled with so much clamor, noise, activity, and interruptions that I am nervous, distressed, and anxious. The nights are so long with so many loud voices or crashes that I cannot sleep or sometimes even relax for long.

I know that Jesus sometimes appeared in strange places to his disciples. Once he came to them in the midst of a storm at sea and brought peace.

Help me to recognize your incarnate presence in the people who come to my bedside by day and by night: physician, nurse, therapist, chaplain, orderly, aide, housekeeper. And calm my nerves and give me peace in the midst of my storm of sickness as you did the disciples on the sea of Galilee.

—RICHARD DAYRINGER

Physician's Prayer

Lord, Who on earth didst minister
    To those who helpless lay
In pain and weakness, hear me now,
    As unto Thee I pray.

Give to mine eyes the power to see
    The hidden source of ill,
Give to my hand the healing touch
    The throb of pain to still.

Grant that mine ears be swift to hear
    The cry of those in pain;
Give to my tongue the words that bring
    Comfort and strength again.

Fill Thou my heart with tenderness,
    My brain with wisdom true
And when in weariness I sink,
    Strengthen Thou me anew.

So in Thy footsteps may I tread,
    Strong in Thy strength always
So may I do Thy blessed work
    And praise Thee day by day.

—AUTHOR UNKNOWN

A Thanksgiving Prayer

Dear God,
    For the ability to sleep or at least rest or relax;
        For appetite, keeping food down, and the ability to drink;
           For freedom from pain or at least its reduction;
                For friends who think of me, send cards, or visit;
                    For the skill and knowledge of my physician, nurse,
                    and the others who treat and care for me;
                    For all who pray for me;
                      And especially for your presence;
From my sickbed I sincerely express my thanks. Amen.

—RICHARD DAYRINGER

A Prayer for Understanding

Eternal and merciful Father;
Thou who dost wait upon us when we are distraught,
And who dost welcome us when we are discomfited,
Give us understanding.
Make us to be humble; make us to be as little children;
Still our spirit in its restlessness,
And make us to be generous with those who have misused us.
Forgive Thou our shortcomings,
For we know we are even more imperfect in Thy sight than we
    are in our own.
Make us to be understanding;
Broaden Thou our intent to forgive;
A lamp set in the midst of bitterness cannot be seen,
But a lamp of generosity gives light unto others.
We thank Thee, our Father, for understanding. Amen.

—RUSSELL DICKS

A Prayer During Pain

Eternal God,
Thou Who dost bear us up in our travail,
And who dost comfort us in our moments of weakness,
Be Thou with this one as she suffers;
Grant her relief from this pain,
And give her patience and fortitude to endure to the end.
Wilt Thou give us peace in Thy presence,
In the quiet of the evening may we come unto Thee,
And in the still morning may we dwell in Thy presence.
As Thy glory shineth in the morning sunrise
May we reflect Thy presence by our faith,
In the name of the Father, the Son, and the Holy Spirit. Amen.

—RUSSELL DICKS

A Prayer for Rest

O God, I am weary with restlessness,
Make me to be still.
Make me to be at peace in my soul,
And my muscles to give over their tension;
Make me to know that as I rest upon my bed,
So I rest in Thee and in Thy support;
In Thy Peace I would abide all the days of my life,
In Thy House would I lie down unto deep slumber
As a guest rests after a weary journey;
And I would dwell in the House of the Lord forever. Amen.

—RUSSELL DICKS